Robert Burns
COUNTRY

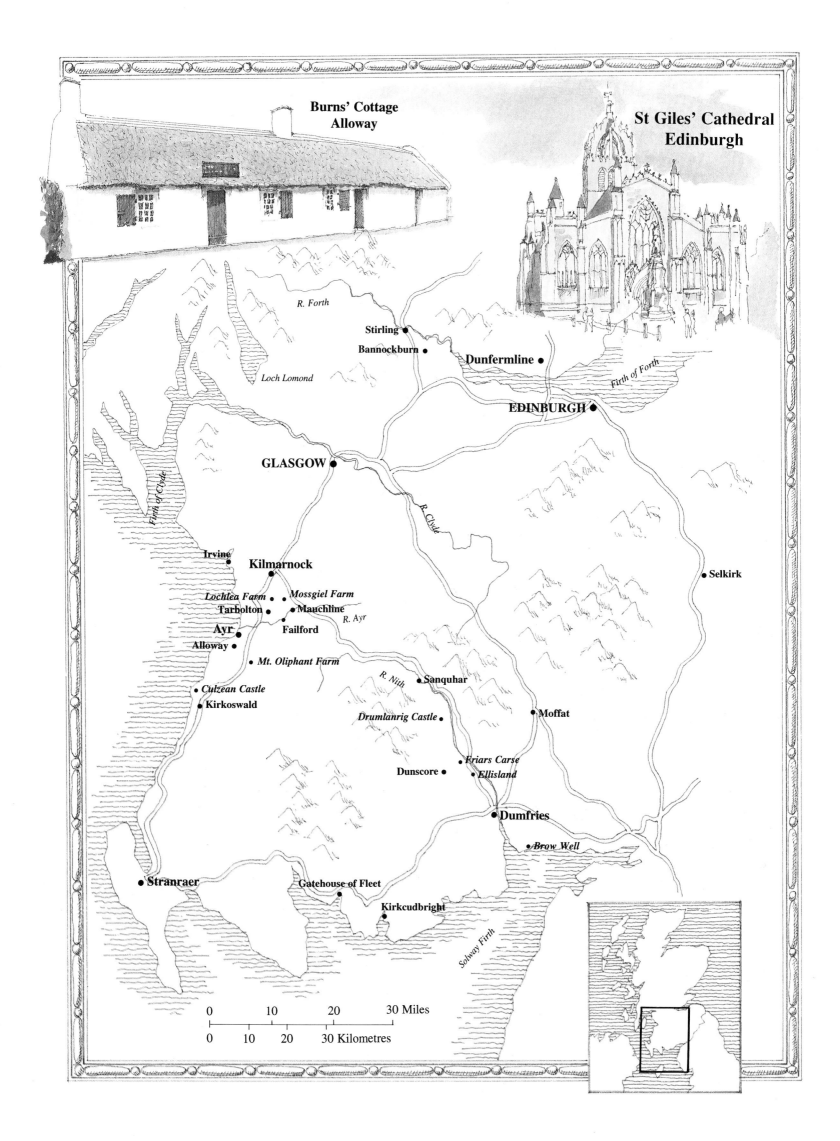

Burns' Cottage
Alloway

St Giles' Cathedral
Edinburgh

R. Forth

Stirling
Bannockburn
Dunfermline

Loch Lomond

Firth of Forth

EDINBURGH

GLASGOW

Firth of Clyde

R. Clyde

Irvine
Kilmarnock

Selkirk

Lochlea Farm
Mossgiel Farm
Tarbolton
Mauchline
R. Ayr
Ayr
Failford
Alloway

Mt. Oliphant Farm

R. Nith
Sanquhar

Culzean Castle
Kirkoswald

Drumlanrig Castle
Moffat

Friars Carse
Dunscore
Ellisland

Dumfries

Brow Well

Stranraer
Gatehouse of Fleet

Kirkcudbright

Solway Firth

0   10   20   30 Miles

0   10   20   30 Kilometres

Robert Burns
COUNTRY

Edmund Swinglehurst

Lomond Books

PHOTOGRAPHIC ACKNOWLEDGMENTS
JACKET FRONT AND BACK MAIN PICTURES:
FRONT COVER: Durisdeer, Near Thornhill, Dumfrieshire.
The Still Moving Picture Co/© Glyn Satterley
BACK COVER: Glentrool Forest, Southern Uplands.
The Still Moving Picture Co/© Glyn Satterley
JACKET FRONT COVER INSETS: Burns' Cottage
The Still Moving Picture Co, Burns' Portrait, Alloway
The Still Moving Picture Co/Doug Corrance

INSIDES
Map: Malcolm Porter
Forbes Magazine Collection, London/The Bridgeman Art
Library, London page 25 top left Robert Burns and
Highland Mary by James Archer (1824-1904).
The Still Moving Picture Co/STB
pages 3, 4-5, 10, 11, (Paul Tomkins 12-13), 13 bottom,
16 top, (Paul Tomkins 18 both, 21 left), 21 right, 23, 24,
27 both, 28 both, 29, 30, 31, 32-33, (Paul Tomkins 49,
57 top), 70, (Paul Tomkins 71, 73), 75 both top, 76 left,
(Paul Tomkins 76 right), 77 bottom.
The Still Moving Picture Co/Doug Corrance
pages 14-15, 20 top, 34, 35 top, 37, 38, 40, 41, 45, 46,
54-55, 68-69, 77 both.

The Still Moving Picture Co/Distant Images
pages 9, 57.
The Still Moving Picture Co/Findlay page 19.
The Still Moving Picture Co/Mika page 20 top left.
The Still Moving Picture Co/Angus Johnson pages 26.
The Still Moving Picture Co/Ken Patterson page 36.
The Still Moving Picture Co/Derek Laird pages 39, 72.
The Still Moving Picture Co/David Robertson
pages 40, 59, 62, 63.
The Still Moving Picture Co/Harvey Wood
pages 44, 51, 52, 58-59, 75 bottom.
The Still Moving Picture Co/Derek Braid page 47.
The Still Moving Picture Co/Pinhole Productions
pages 64-65, 79.
The Still Moving Picture Co/Val Bissland 66-67.
The Still Moving Picture Co/Glyn Satterley page 78.
Roy Davidson pages 8, 13 top, 16 top and bottom right,
17, 25 right.
Scottish National Portrait Gallery
page 7: Portrait of Robert Burns
by Alexander Nasmyth 1828.
Page 22: Inauguration of Burns
Page 35: Burns at Lord Monboddo's

Published in 1996 by
Lomond Books
36 West Shore Road,
Granton, Edinburgh
EH5 1QD

ISBN 1 85361 440 8

**Copyright © 1996 Regency House Publishing
Limited**

Designed by Annabel Trodd

Printed in China

CONTENTS

INTRODUCTION

Robert Burns has a precise and particular significance in the literature and history of the Scottish people. He was born in Ayrshire in 1759, only fourteen years after the defeat of Bonnie Prince Charlie at Culloden had ended hopes of a Stuart restoration and, more significantly, destroyed the Highland clan system.

After their victory at Culloden, the British government under William Pitt, later Lord Chatham, set about transforming Scotland from a country where clan loyalties could divide as much as they could unite into one nation within Great Britain. Many Scotsmen, albeit reluctantly, were prepared to go along with this, but most regretted the loss of the essentially Scottish culture and traditions which were beginning to disappear under rule from London.

Culloden had been more than a defeat for the Stuarts and the Highland clans; it left a psychological wound which was difficult to heal. Destiny gave Robbie Burns the role of healer.

From his earliest years in Alloway Robert Burns heard songs and stories which had been passed down orally for generations. They fired his imagination and gave him a sense of his roots and a feeling of being part of the culture of his people. As he grew up he also began to collect the songs and stories and to use them in his poetry. He began writing poetry when he was still a schoolboy, making great use of Lallans, the dialect of southern Scotland which was almost a second language and which he heard being used by ordinary folk in their everyday speech.

He began the habit, which lasted throughout his life, of jotting down words in his journals and commonplace books as he heard them, carefully adding definitions: 'Whope, a glen between two hills – Parreck, to force a ewe to Mother an alien lamb by closing them up together,' he scribbled at the end of the journal of his Borders tour, among notes on mileages covered and monies due.

When his poems were first published in Kilmarnock in 1786 in a modest book intended for friends, he included a glossary of all the Lallans words used in them. *Poems, Chiefly in the Scottish Dialect* became an overnight success because they expressed the hidden thoughts of Scottish people, not only simple folk like Burns' family but the high and mighty who found Burns' passionate love of all things Scottish close to their own hearts.

Burns was also a man of his time in a broader sense for, whether he was aware of it or not, he personified the Natural Man written about by the philosopher Jean Jacques Rousseau, who believed that man's natural goodness had been corrupted by institutionalized life. This idea, which developed into the Romantic view of life and the worship of Nature, was current in the cultured society of Scotland whose members lionized the poetical ploughman from Ayr when he arrived in Edinburgh.

But Burns was no ignorant peasant. His father had done his best to provide his son with a good education, though it was not a regular and systematic one, and Burns, who was a voracious reader, had filled in the gaps.

His literary accomplishment and his social skills — he was a fine dancer and a better conversationalist — made him very acceptable in Edinburgh society. The fifteen-year-old Walter Scott encountered him at a party in Edinburgh and, many years later, recalled the man: '... There was a strong expression of sense and shrewdness in all his lineaments; the eye alone, I think, indicated the poetical character and temperament. It was large and of a dark cast, which glowed, I say literally glowed, when he spoke with feeling or interest. I never saw such another eye in a human head, though I have seen the most distinguished men of my time.'

Even so, Burns the natural man was more at ease in inns and ale houses, or spending evenings in the drinking clubs of Edinburgh, where the whisky flowed and the conversation was lively and Burns could declaim his anti-establishment views and bawdy poetry. It was not long, however, before these anti-establishment views, along with his fatal susceptibility to pretty women, usually servants or country lasses, which led to numerous unwanted pregnancies, brought upon him the censure of the strict and narrowminded Scottish Kirk as well as the distrust of respectable society.

But Burns' natural instincts were also the source of his creative imagination and had he managed to control them and become a respectable citizen the world might well have lost one of its great lyric poets whose work produced quotable lines second only to Shakespeare in quantity and quality, and who could write with equal passion about his view of life, his love of women and his love of nature, from superb scenery to humble creatures like a mouse or even a louse.

Every year, on 25 January, his birthday, Robbie Burns is remembered and his life celebrated in many parts of the world, where there are Scots or their descendants, and even where there are not.

Wherever the Burns Night party, the toasts will undoubtedly be from the poet's own immortal works – accompanied by his favourite libation, whisky. Someone may sing *Auld Lang Syne*, though they will almost certainly have sung it as recently as Hogmanay (New Year's Eve), and someone will say 'A man's a man for a' that' and perhaps even go on to the verse which explains why Robbie Burns is so beloved by so many:

'For a' that, an' a' that,
It's comin' yet for a' that,
That man to man the world o'er
Shall brother be for a' that.'

Alexander Nasmyth painted this portrait 32 years after the death of Robert Burns. He painted from life sketches made when the poet was staying in Edinburgh in the winter of 1786-1787.
The portrait is now one of the treasures of the National Gallery of Scotland in Edinburgh.

GROWING UP IN AYRSHIRE

Robert Burns said of Ayr that it was a place 'wham ne'er a town surpasses, For honest men and bonie lasses'. Ayr repaid the compliment by erecting this fine statue to the poet in 1891. It stands in Burns Statue Square in front of the railway station. Ayr was the nearest large town to Alloway and William and Agnes Burnes had their eldest son, Robert, baptized in Ayr's Auld Kirk, also called the New Church of St John.

The south-west corner of Scotland, with its rolling hills and uplands and attractive sea coast given a mild climate by the Gulf Stream, seems at first sight an unlikely country to have produced a passionate and radical-minded poet. A more romantic and suitable background for Robert Burns, Scotland's finest lyric poet, would have been, perhaps, the western Highlands with their long mysterious lochs and impressive mountains once inhabited by wild clansmen jealous of their independence and constantly at war with each other.

But it was the south-west county of Ayrshire, today part of Strathclyde, which saw the birth of Robert Burns on 25 January 1759. The Ayrshire into which Robert Burns was born was a countryside of rolling hill farms, much as today, where making a living was not easy, especially if your family had little money; it was also a land steeped in myth and legend, in which story and song preserved an ancient grass-roots culture which was to fire the childhood imagination of Robert Burns.

Robert's father, William Burnes, who retained the 'e' of the older spelling of the family's name, was a gardener from the north-east of Scotland who had moved to the south-west in search of work. The place he chose for the future home of his family was Alloway, a small village near Ayr on the River Doon. Here, he built a small thatched cottage where he and his wife, Agnes Broun, could raise a family.

The first of their six children, Robert, was born in this cottage and lived for the first seven years of his life in it, absorbing the historic atmosphere of Ayr, where William Wallace, who was born at Ellerslie, near Paisley, and was therefore counted as a local hero, had once defied the English, burning 500 of them in barns where they were sheltering; where Robert the Bruce later destroyed a castle rather than have it fall into the hands of the English; and where even Oliver Cromwell had seen the advantages of building a fort. Like the Bruce's castle, Cromwell's fort is long gone, although reminders of it in Ayr today remain in place names like Fort Street and Citadel Place. Ayr, therefore, was a place with heroic echoes which were to ring in young Robbie Burns' mind, arousing a fiery patriotism which later provided one of the great themes of his poetry; the countryside in which he toiled gave his writing the strong and compassionate feeling for nature which was another vital strand in his work.

William and Agnes Burnes produced a hard-working family in the impoverished Scotland of the time. William worked in the fine gardens of the Lord Provost of Ayr and his wife Agnes had a job in the dairy. Though hardly comfortable, the family home in Alloway seems to have been a happy place. Young Robert spent hours sitting by candlelight in the smoke-filled room, often shared with the family's farm animals, listening to the traditional songs his mother, who was illiterate, had learned from her own parents and to the stories told by his mother's friend Sarah Davidson.

Some of the stories may well have been their versions of the old myths and legends of the area. Particularly thrilling

would be the story of Maggie Osborne, the Witch of Ayr. Legend had it that she was one of several women burned as witches near the Fish Cross in Ayr's market place. Maggie Osborne's crimes were said to have been so dreadful that she could only have carried them out with the help of the Devil. She was said to have left her home in Ayr on a broomstick many times, flying over the Carrick Hills to Galloway, working her devilish spells on the way: you would be able to tell where she had stopped because of the dry patches left in the grass on the hills by the feet of the imps of Hell, her regular familiars.

The Carrick Hills, which lie to the south-west of Ayr and Alloway and rise to 287 metres (932 feet) at Brown Carrick Hill, were much the same quiet, grass-and turf-covered rolling hill country, populated largely by grazing sheep and cattle, in

Robert Burns' day as they are now; even so, there would be enough of an atmosphere in their very quiet to stir a lively boy's imagination....

Alloway's ruined church, Kirk Alloway, would have been another stimulus to the young Robert's imagination. It was a favourite spot for William Burnes, who often took his small son there when he was trying to rebuild the ruined walls. William Burnes was a deeply religious man, passing his uncompromising faith on to his son who, as he grew up, did not hesitate to criticize the hypocrisy and corruption he saw in the narrow Calvinism of the Kirk.

William also believed in the importance of a good education and from early on made sure that his sons received whatever schooling was available. At first, this was at a school in Alloway Mill but when the

The neat white-washed and thatched cottage in Alloway which the visitor retracing Burns' life sees today is a much improved and redecorated version of the simple mud cottage which William Burnes built for his family. Here, the family, including six children, lived close together, sharing their cramped quarters with farm animals. Here Robbie Burns studied by candlelight and listened to his mother, who was illiterate, singing the songs and ballads which had been passed down through generations of her family and recounting many local legends and tales of such heroes as William Wallace.

teacher left he was not replaced, as according to 17th-century Acts of Parliament, which provided for schools in every parish, he should have been.

Undeterred by the lack of any official action in the matter, William Burnes persuaded some of his neighbours to contribute to the pay of a teacher from Ayr. This was one John Murdoch, recommended by William's friends at the Ayr Academy, and a contract was made with him at Simpson's Inn in Ayr.

With Murdoch's help the sons of five Alloway cottagers, including five-year-old Robert Burns and, later, his brother Gilbert, learned to read and write, to spell correctly and to parse sentences. Among their schoolbooks were the Bible, Masons's collection of prose and verse and Fisher's English Grammar. Robert and Gilbert were among the most talented of Murdoch's pupils. In his reminiscences, Murdoch later recalled that the elder brother, Robert, was serious, contemplative and had a thoughtful mind but an 'untunable voice'; Gilbert, on the other hand, could sing in tune and was the most likely of the two to 'court the muses'.

Robert was taking in everything that he was taught and more besides. His memories of this period of his life included the *Vision of Mirza*, Addison's poetry, including the hymn, *How are thy servants blest, Oh Lord*, a *Life of Hannibal* and *The History of Sir William Wallace* . The lives of military heroes inspired him as they did most small boys and whenever recruiting units appeared with drums and fife to persuade Ayrshire men to join the British Army Robert would run after them and march with them. But most of all he was inspired by William Wallace and his struggle for Scottish independence. Wallace, he wrote later, 'poured a Scottish prejudice into my veins which will boil along there till the floodgates of life shut in eternal rest.'

In 1766 William Burnes applied to his employer in Alloway for the lease of a 70-acre farm at Mount Oliphant, two miles east of Alloway, which he was granted. Here, the family were to be in more commodious circumstances, though the work became no easier. Robert and Gilbert now had to walk over two miles to school, a pleasant enough journey in summer, but

The clean, bright interior of the Burns Cottage in Alloway today, filled with furniture and domestic china of the period, gives little idea of the true conditions in which Burns' family struggled for a living in an unyielding environment and in almost feudal conditions. Although this was the usual way of life for the bulk of the peasant farming class of his time, Robert Burns, a rebel at heart, never accepted it. Again and again, he used his poetry to criticize what he saw as the corruption and hypocrisy of people who wanted to preserve the existing order, including the Kirk, with its habit of calling those who broke its laws or defaulted by ignoring their religious 'duty' to account for their sins before the whole congregation.

more arduous in winter, especially as the boys were expected to work on the farm when they were not at school.

The farm was beautifully situated on a hill with views of the coast and sea but it soon became evident that the soil was poor and that even with the whole family working on it, it would not pay its way. Despite the difficulties, William Burnes was still concerned with the boys' education and ensured that Robert continued studying with his teacher Murdoch, who had now returned to Ayr. French and Latin were included in their studies.

Robert was 15 when he received his first taste of one of the pleasures of life which would inspire his poetry and also bring him troubles galore. At harvest time it was customary to pair men and women to share the work and Robert found himself paired with a young 14-year-old called Nelly Kirkpatrick. 'A bonie, sweet, sonsie lass', he wrote later. 'She, unwittingly to herself, initiated me in a certain delicious Passion, which in spite of Acid Disappointment, Gin horse Prudence and bookworm Philosophy, I hold to be the first of human joys, our dearest pleasure here below.'

His awakening to the delights of love were innocent, however, for 'gin horse Prudence' held him back from an active pursuit and seduction of the young woman who had aroused his passion. Instead, he poured his feelings into one of his first songs, *Tis this is Nelly pleases me*, inspired by hearing Nelly singing as she worked in the fields. Then, too, his father chose this time to send him to school in Kirkoswald, the new surroundings giving the young man many new experiences to savour.

Although he may have now moved away from the immediate vicinity of Alloway and Ayr, the influence of his early years there remained important to Robert Burns all his life, just as the poet himself remains a potent force in Ayr today.

Ayr and the countryside surrounding the town may have changed greatly since Burns' time, but there is still much that he would recognize. Alloway itself has become a suburb of Ayr rather than a village in its own right, but the cottage William Burnes built and in which Robert was born is still there, at the heart both of the village and of the major tourist industry that has been built up round the memory of Robert Burns.

While Ayrshire has several strings to its tourism bow, not least its attractive coast of sandy beaches and superb golf courses, including Troon and Prestwick to the north and Turnberry to the south of Ayr, the Robert Burns factor is of paramount importance.

All places with which he can be associated in Alloway have been gathered together in the Burns National Heritage Park, established in 1995 and much promoted by the local tourist board. Most recent of the attractions in the Burns National Heritage Park is the Tam O' Shanter Experience Visitor Centre, opened by the Queen in 1995, and named after the hero of one of Robert Burns' most popular poems, *Tam O' Shanter*.

Tam O' Shanter is a rollicking poem

Formerly the Land o' Burns Centre in Alloway, this modern building, with a new theatre using all the latest high-tech multimedia techniques, is now at the heart of the Tam o' Shanter Experience Visitor Centre in Alloway. The Centre, in the newly formed Burns National Heritage Park, was opened by the Queen in 1995, in time to be a main focus of the International Burns Festival in 1996, celebrating the poet's life and work on the bicentenary of his death.

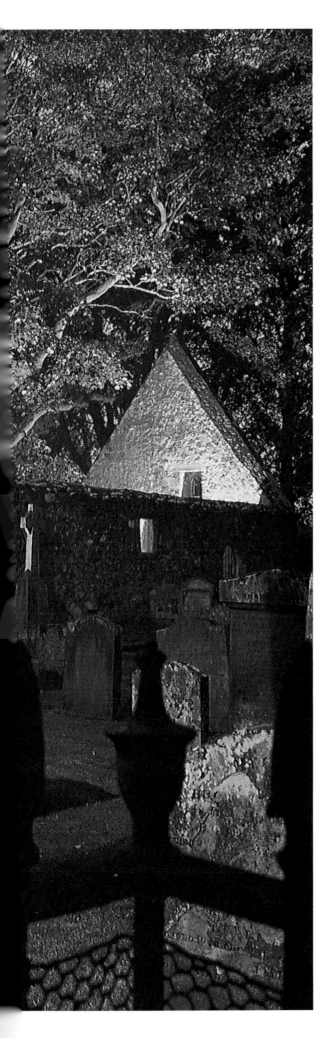

about witches and the evils of drink. Tam o' Shanter, riding home from Ayr on his grey mare Meg after a convivial evening with his friend Souter Johnnie (in what is today called the Tam O' Shanter Inn in High Street, Alloway), happened to glance through a window into the Auld Kirk at Alloway – 'And, wow! Tam saw an unco [wondrous] sight!': witches and warlocks dancing 'Nae cotillion, brent new frae France, But hornpipes, jigs, strathspeys and reels' under the eye of Auld Nick himself. Among them, wide-eyed Tam noticed, was a bonnie lass wearing only a cutty sark (a short shift). Unfortunately, Tam drew attention to himself and had to flee from the angry witches and warlocks. Knowing they could not follow him over water, Tam fled towards the Auld Brig o' Doon and had nearly made it to safety when one of the witches – winsome Nannie of the 'cutty sark' – grabbed at Meg's tail, pulling it off. And the moral of the story? The last verse of the poem sums it up:

> *'Now, wha this tale o' truth shall read,*
> *Ilk man, and mother's son, take heed:*
> *Whene'er to drink you are inclin'd,*
> *Or cutty sarks rin in your mind,*
> *Think! ye may buy the joys o'er dear:*
> *Remember Tam o' Shanter's meare.'*

While Tam o' Shanter and his 'ancient, trusty, drouthy cronie', Souter Johnnie were based on real men whom Burns knew well – Douglas Graham of Shanter Farm and John Davidson, a village souter (cobbler) in Kirkoswald – it is perhaps not too unlikely that the witches were inspired by the witches of Ayr told about in song and story round the fireside in Alloway.

Now Tam o' Shanter and the witches live again at the heart of a thoroughly 20th-century high-tech multimedia presentation used to take visitors back to the Ayrshire of Robert Burns' time.

ABOVE
The grave of Robert Burns' father, William at Alloway's Auld Kirk. Also remembered on the gravestone is Burns' mother, Agnes, who outlived him by nearly twenty-five years.

OPPOSITE
The ruins of Alloway Auld Kirk, the spotlighting suggesting how the kirk might have looked to Tam o' Shanter when he spotted witches and warlocks dancing in the kirk under the eye of Old Nick.

BELOW
A 19th-century playbill highlighting a performance of Robert Burns' famous poem *Tam o' Shanter*. Today, at the Tam o' Shanter Experience in Alloway all the latest multimedia techniques are used to retell the rollicking tale.

PAGES 14-15
The Auld Brig o' Doon in its pretty setting over the River Doon in Alloway retains the romantic atmosphere of the bridge at the heart of Tam o' Shanter's story. Tam was able to ride hell for leather over the bridge; today, the bridge is open only to walkers.

BELOW
The elegantly classical Burns Monument in Alloway. Perhaps a little inappropriate as a memorial to someone of Burns' down-to-earth reputation, it remains a conspicuous landmark, offering fine views over the country Burns knew well.

Also within the bounds of the National Heritage Park are the haunted ruins of Kirk Alloway itself, central to the story of Tam o' Shanter and also of great interest to Burns' followers because his father, William Burnes, is buried in the graveyard. A short walk away, the Auld Brig o' Doon, over which Tam was chased by the witches, crosses the Doon river. From the crest of the high-arched bridge, which today is restricted to walkers, there is a fine view of the river and its wooded banks. The woods on the far side of the bridge are within the boundary of the old Doon estate, where William Burnes worked as a gardener.

The thatched cottage in which Robert Burns was born has been recently restored to such a gleaming, white-washed, neatly thatched perfection that Robert Burns might, indeed, have some difficulty recognizing his first home. Inside, the cottage allows visitors to experience what life was like in Burns' time, with a short audio-visual presentation bringing to life the sights and sounds of the farmhouse.

Besides Burns' Cottage is the Museum, with a fine display of memorabilia and a wide-ranging collection of books, manuscripts, artefacts and paint-

ings connected with the poet and his work.

The last element in the Burns National Heritage Park is the Grecian-style Burns Monument, set in attractive gardens. The Monument, opened in 1823, is a conspicuous landmark, offering superb views over the country Robert Burns knew so well, including the wooded 'banks and braes o' Bonnie Doon' where the Burns children ran happily barefoot, the churchyard of the Auld Kirk and the Auld Brig o' Doon.

While the large and busy centre of Ayr lies outside the Burns National Heritage Park, it still offers much of interest to people following in the footsteps of Robert Burns, who himself described Ayr in *Tam O' Shanter* as being a place 'wham ne'er a town surpasses, For honest men and bonie lasses'.

Burns was baptized in the Auld Kirk, off the High Street. This church is also known as the New Church of St John because it was built in 1654-6 with money given by Oliver Cromwell to compensate for his absorption into his great fort of the old church, which he had converted into an armoury.

There is a good view from the church-yard of Ayr's Auld Brig, built in the 13th century and for 500 years the town's only bridge. After the New Bridge was built in 1788, Burns wrote a poetic 'dialogue', *The Twa Brigs*, in which he poured scorn on the poor qualities of the Auld Brig. In the roadway opposite the south end of the Auld Brig a cross of stones marks the site of the Fish Cross, where the witches of Ayr were burned. (The New Bridge one sees today is not the bridge of Burns' time, for it was rebuilt in 1877.)

Near the New Bridge, in Boat Vennel, is Loudoun Hall, a fine merchant's house of the 15th century, and the oldest house in Ayr. While Robert Burns may have known Loudoun Hall, he certainly did not know Ayr's railway station. This is where you must go, however, to see Ayr's fine bronze statue of the poet, in a square named after him in front of the railway station. Designed by Morrison Hunter and sculpted by G. E. Lawson, the statue was unveiled in 1891.

Kirkoswald, to which Robert Burns was sent for the summer of 1775 to study surveying and mensuration, is south of Ayr, 4 miles from the historic town of Maybole, seat of the earls of Cassillis who were head of the powerful Lowland fami-ly, the Kennedys. Kirkoswald itself, with its white-washed houses set right up against the pavements of the streets, is typ-ical of Lowland Scottish villages built in the late 17th and 18th centuries. It is not far from the coast, indented with bays and beaches which today shelter resorts and fine golf links but which in earlier cen-turies provided havens for smugglers – hence its nickname, the Smugglers Coast. In the late 18th century, the small popula-tion lived off the sea as well as off the unyielding land.

This was a new world for young Burns who until now had lived very much among farming folk – and few enough of those because of his hard and busy life. At

Kirkoswald he joined in the social life cen-tred on the inns of the place and met the rough seafaring men of the village when-ever he could escape from the supervison of his mother's brother, with whom he was staying at a farm, Ballochneil, a mile outside Kirkoswald. At Ballochneil he shared a room with a young man, William Niven, who had already discovered the tavern life of Kirkoswald and Maybole and who quickly introduced the young farming lad to both.

Among the people Burns came to know in Kirkoswald was a cobbler (or 'souter'), John Davidson, model for Souter Johnnie, Tam o' Shanter's cronie. John Davidson's thatched cottage, called 'Souter Johnnie's Cottage', is now in the care of the National Trust for Scotland. It is beautifully cared for and well worth a visit for it contains many relics of the souter and his craft as well as a collection of Burnsiana. In a restored ale house in the garden are life-size figures of Souter Johnnie, Tam o' Shanter, the inn keeper in Ayr and his wife, sitting, as Burns described them, 'by the ingle bleezing brightly... ae market nicht'.

Douglas Graham, who farmed a local farm, Shanter Farm, and who inspired the character of Tam o' Shanter, is buried in

ABOVE
Modern farming methods have made life for the farmers of Ayreshire easier than in the days when Robert Burns, his father and his brother toiled on land like this near Alloway. Mount Oliphant farm, to which the Burns family moved when Robert Burns was seven, was just two miles from Alloway.

OPPOSITE, BELOW RIGHT
The Tam o' Shanter Inn in Ayr, well-known to Robert Burns, was where he chose to put Tam o' Shanter and his friend Souter Johnnie as they rather overdid their drinking before Tam set off home, encountering witches in Alloway Auld Kirk on the way. The carefully preserved inn is today a Robert Burns museum.

OPPOSITE, TOP
The Auld Brig' at Ayr was built in the 13th century. For 500 years it was the town's only bridge.

the churchyard at Kirkoswald, while the site of the school Burns attended there is now filled by a hotel called, naturally enough, the Shanter Hotel. A bronze plaque on the wall recalls Burns' connection with the former school.

The school Burns attended in Kirkoswald was run by Hugh Rodger, who advanced Robert's knowledge of mathematics and other sciences while teaching him surveying. Next to the school lived a pretty young woman called Peggy Thomson; soon Burns was experiencing the same feelings that Nelly Kirkpatrick had aroused in him earlier in the year. 'She...rapidly took my mind off Trigonometry and set it at a Tangent,' Burns wrote later. 'I struggled with my Sines and Co-Sines, Like Proserpine gathering flowers. Herself a fair flower...'.

By now Robbie Burns was discovering in himself the power to use words to create imaginative and persuasive images.

The country round Kirkoswald in which Burns spent the summer of 1775 studying and also discovering much about himself has in many respects remained unchanged. The romantic, legend-surrounded castles built on the coastal cliffs are still there, as are the towns and villages Burns knew, though many of the latter

have recent housing estates spreading out into the surrounding countryside. The largest town in the area, then as now, was the coastal town of Girvan. Now a seaside resort with a fine seafront, Girvan is set at the mouth of the Water of Girvan, a pretty river whose valley is dotted with castellated tower houses, including the impressive 16th-century Killochan Castle, and ancient villages like Dailly, Crosshill and Kirkmichael. Robert the Bruce once held court at Girvan; later, in a different context, so did William Bell Scott who gathered about him many of the leading Pre-Raphaelites at his castellated home, Perskill Castle.

Ten miles off the shore from Girvan is Ailsa Craig, a famous 341.5-metre (1110-feet) rock outcrop which is an important nesting site for birds. In his well-known song, *Duncan Gray cam here to woo,* Burns described Meg, the object of Duncan's wooing, as being as 'deaf as Ailsa Craig' to his prayers. The lonely rock once belonged to Crossraguel Abbey, whose evocative ruins stand on the inland road between Kirkoswald and Maybole and were passed many times by Robbie Burns and William Niven as they walked to Maybole – a livelier place then Kirkoswald.

Crossraguel Abbey, founded in 1244, was a Cluniac house powerful enough in its great days to mint its own coins. Even by the 16th century it was important enough for the local great lord, Gilbert, 4th Earl of Cassilis, to cast an acquisitive eye over it. The story of his attempt to wrest the abbey lands from its Commendator, one Alan Stewart – whom he roasted in soap in the dungeon of his grim castle, Dunure in September, 1570 in an unsuccessful attempt to get Stewart to sign over the abbey lands to him – was one of the great tales of the area, all the more striking for being true. (Alan Stewart was eventually released by his kinsman, Stewart of Bargany, who sent a rescue party to

Dunure from his castle, Killochan.)

No doubt Robert Burns, who was now beginning to collect the tales and legends of Ayrshire, knew the story of the roasting of the Commendator and also knew the story, by now surrounded by myth, of the end of the wicked Earl of Cassilis. Despite being called before James VI's Privy Council to explain his actions, Earl Gilbert was fined but otherwise went unpunished and seemed to suffer no remorse. Local people who reckoned that the Devil had marked Earl Gilbert for his own felt themselves vindicated when the earl was thrown from his horse and killed a few years later. A crow flew onto his coffin as it was being pulled to Maybole for his burial and the horses were unable to move forward until it flew off. By this time, of course, the Devil had already claimed Earl Gilbert's soul. The previous evening, the master of a ship sailing out of the Firth of Clyde had seen a great fiery chariot coming out of the setting sun towards him. 'Whence and whither bound?' the ship's master shouted out; 'From Hell to Cassilis for the soul of the Earl', had come the ghostly reply.

Today, Dunure Castle is a ruin, dominating a headland south of the village of Dunure, whose tiny harbour is all that is left of the former fishing industry here. For centuries, Dunure lived off fishing and also what was called the 'Arran water' trade – in other words, whisky smuggling.

Burns probably knew both Dunure Castle and Culzean Castle, another great

Even on a brilliantly sunny day, the ruins of Dunure Castle, set on a headland overlooking the Firth of Clyde, have a grim aspect. Mary, Queen of Scots, making a royal progress, spent a night here in 1563; just seven years later Gilbert, Earl of Cassilis roasted the Commendator of Crossragruel Abbey in the castle's dungeon in an attempt to make him hand over the abbey's rich lands to the earl. The attempt failed, and Earl Gilbert, apart from a fine, went unpunished.

ABOVE
Sunset at Girvan, the popular resort at the mouth of the Water of Girvan. Its sheltered waters attracts the boating fraternity. For Robert Burns, Girvan's attraction was the livelieness of its fishing and trading community, which added a boisterous conviviality to the town's many inns.

RIGHT
Culzean Castle, on the Ayrshire coast south of Ayr, belonged, like Dunure, to the earls of Cassilis. The castle that Robert Burns knew underwent a transformation at the hands of the Scottish architect, Robert Adam, in the years after Burns left the area, so he may never have known what is now one of the finest Adam houses in Scotland.

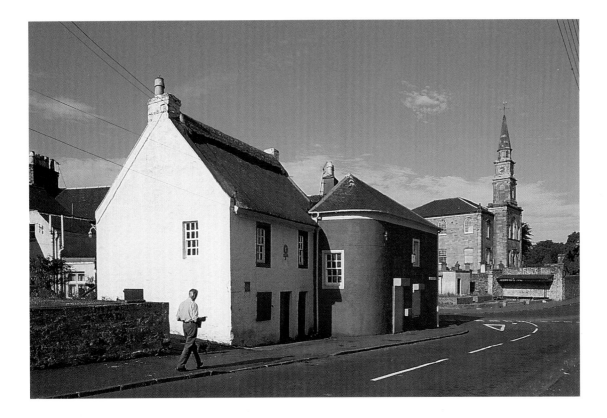

castle of the Earls of Cassilis which is also on the coast, overlooking the Firth of Clyde at the southern end of Culzean Bay. Two years after Burns left Kirkoswald, the great Scottish architect, Robert Adam began rebuilding Culzean Castle for the 10th Earl of Cassilis, creating what is today one of the finest Adam houses in Scotland around the old Kennedy tower castle which Burns would have known.

Culzean Castle is one of the glories of the National Trust for Scotland. In the splendid interior Adam installed an impressive oval staircase and a magnificent drawing room whose plaster ceilings are much admired by visitors to the castle. The more recent history of the castle links it to General Eisenhower who was given the use of an apartment for his lifetime, an event which is commemorated in the Eisenhower Presentation in the castle. The 560-acre park which surrounds Culzean Castle was the first country park to be opened in Scotland and offers several miles of fine country walks and nature trails; you can reach them from the car park by the Castle or from Maidens village to the south, which begins with a walk along the beach to the estate's gate.

Drivers taking the main road from Culzean north to Dunure should be prepared for an unusual 'entertainment': the 'Electric Brae' (correct name Croy Brae), about five miles north of Culzean, where the configuration of the surrounding landscape creates the optical illusion that you are going downhill when, in fact, you are going up.

After his summer at Kirkoswald, Burns returned to the family's farm at Mount Oliphant for one last, hard winter. Then in 1777 came a move to a new farm which William Burnes had leased at Lochlea, near Tarbolton, lying in farming country seven and a half miles north-west of Ayr, near the Water of Fail. Lochlea, which can be found today in the country east of Tarbolton, on a minor road off the B744, proved to be a bad choice for William Burnes to have made. It demanded an enormous amount of work for a poor yield from sour land. This meant that the whole family had to work hard to make ends meet and Robert was hard put to keep up with his studies. There was little relaxation in this kind of life but

Robert, who had become fond of a gregarious social life after his time at Kirkoswald, escaped whenever he could to nearby Tarbolton and Mauchline.

While Mauchline has grown into a town, Tarbolton today remains very much a village. Here, in a 17th-century thatched house, 18-year-old Robert, his brother Gilbert and several friends founded the Bachelors' Club, a debating society in which they discussed many issues of the day, serious and not-so-serious, including such topics as whether it was better to marry a rich farmer's daughter or a plain, sensible and loving girl. The house, which was also used for dancing classes – greatly enjoyed by the Burns brothers – was where Robert Burns took his first degrees in Freemasonry. Eventually, he became Deputy Master of the St James Lodge in Tarbolton.

The Bachelors' Club is now in the care of the National Trust for Scotland, who keep a fine display of Burns relics in it to interest visitors.

While there are few other connections in Tarbolton with Burns' life at Lochlea Farm, where the family lived until 1784 – the church, for instance, dates from 1821 and the miners' cottages on the edge of the village came much later in the 19th century – a walk to Leglan (or Laighland) Wood outside the town is of interest for it follows in Burns' footsteps. He went there often because this was the place from which his hero, William Wallace, had watched the burning of the Ayr barns; a cairn now marks where Burns walked.

In 1781, while the Burns family was still at Lochlea, Robert took time away from the arduous life of the farm (and from his courtship of a girl called Alison Begbie) to learn about flax-dressing in the old town and port of Irvine, several miles north of Ayr. Today Irvine, an industrial port and 'new town' on the shores of the Firth of Clyde, is promoted, with the three towns of Saltcoats, Ardrossan and Stevenston, as a leisure area in Ayrshire, with excellent leisure centres, including the Magnum Centre in Irvine, a fine country park at Kilwinning, and good museums, including the Scottish Maritime Museum, where the collection of tugs and Clyde puffers (of the kind immortalized in the classic Ealing comedy, *The Maggie*), is a big attraction.

In late 18th-century Irvine Robert Burns found a bustling town, already growing in importance as a port for Glasgow and beginning to exploit local coal resources. Here, he met the same kind of rough sea-going folk he had known at Kirkoswald, along with merchants and other itinerant workers with a wider experience of the world than his own.

Irvine also appealed to him because of its history; William Wallace had been let down here by his supporters who had made a secret deal with the English, and Mary, Queen of Scots had stayed at the 14th-century Seagate Castle, now a ruin, in 1563; Irvine still holds its Marymass Week every August to commemorate her visit. The seven months that Robert Burns spent in Irvine learning the trade of flax-dressing added their own footnote to the history of the town, for everything came to a climax when the house he was living in went up in flames at a particularly boisterous Hogmanay party during which a great deal of the new blended whisky from Kilmarnock had been drunk. It was for just such occasions that Robbie Burns wrote *Auld Lang Syne* (Scottish dialect for 'old long ago'), the song without which no Hogmanay (or New Year's Eve for non-Scots) is complete:

'Should auld acquaintance be forgot,
And never brought to mind?
Should auld acquaintance be forgot,
And days o' auld lang syne?

And for auld lang syne, my jo,
For auld lang syne,
We'll tak a cup o' kindness yet,
For auld lang syne.'

Irvine's Glasgow Vennel Museum, set in a cobbled street in a 19th-century building, includes on its site the thatched Heckling Shop where Burns learned to dress flax. Burns' Lodgings, also on the museum site, is a reconstruction of the room where Burns lived.

Perhaps of greater interest to Burns' followers is the Burns Club and Museum in Eglinton Street in Irvine. Founded in 1826, this is the oldest continuous Burns Club in the world. Among the museum's treasures are original manuscripts of poems included in the famous Kilmarnock edition. The Porthead Tavern, on the corner of Glasgow Vennel and the High Street, is of interest, too, for in 1781 it was the home of Provost Charles Hamilton of Craiglaw, who befriended Robert Burns when he first came to Irvine and later helped him arrange the publication of his poems.

The burning of the flax shop left Burns without a reason for staying in Irvine and he returned to Lochlea, where his father was having a long-drawn-out legal wrangle with David McClure, the man from whom he had leased the farm. The hard work on the unproductive land and his anxiety about the outcome of his disagreement with McClure had sapped the old man's energy. In February 1784, just two weeks after the Court of Session upheld his case, William Burnes died, leaving Robert to take over the role of head of the poverty-stricken family.

OPPOSITE
The Inauguration of Burns as a Freemason. He was a member of the St James' Lodge at Tarbolton.

ABOVE
In 1781, Burns took time off from working on his father's farm at Lochlea to learn flax-dressing in Irvine, living in a house in this street, Glasgow Vennel. Burns found life in Irvine, a quiet but busy seaport, to his liking.

The Heckling Shop, now on the site of Irvine's Glasgow Vennel Museum, where Burns learned the trade of flax-dressing.

POEMS, CHIEFLY IN THE SCOTTISH DIALECT

Mossgiel Farm, near Mauchline, today. Although it is still very much a working farm, it may be visited and has a small museum devoted to Burns. The buildings shown in this photograph are not the farm buildings Robert Burns and his brother Gilbert knew, for they were rebuilt after the Burns brothers' time there in the mid-1780s. Although the land here was better than at the family's previous farm, Lochlea, Robert and Gilbert Burns proved no more successful at farming it profitably.

William Burnes' death brought about great changes in Robert Burns' life. He was now free of his father's restraining influence, which had expressed itself in disapproval of many of the young man's activities, from dancing classes to flirting with girls – a disapproval which Robert Burns was to blame for much of his own later dissipations. For some time before their father's death, Robert and Gilbert Burns had been secretly considering the possibility of leaving Lochlea for a better farm. The successful end of the litigation with McClure now enabled them to turn thought into action and they leased from a Mauchline lawyer and friend, Gavin Hamilton, a farm at Mossgiel, a mile north-west of Mauchline. For a rent of £90 a year, the Burns family now had a comfortable home on reasonable farming land. That Robert Burns thought highly of Gavin Hamilton is clear from his poem *A Dedication: to Gavin Hamilton Esq.*:

> '*Expect na, Sir, in this narration,*
> *A fleechin, fleth'rin Dedication,*
> *To roose you up, an' ca' you guid...*'

This was a sign of the maturing poet whose dedicatory poems were never mere empty praise and who felt that in offering a gift of his creative self he owed no man anything.

With the move to Mossgiel Farm, the focus of attention in 'Burns Country' moves to Mauchline, a farming town east of Ayr which is today almost as important a part of Scotland for Burns enthusiasts as Ayr/Alloway. It was not just that

Mauchline was a lively town, with a number of inns and a tradition of entertaining in the homes of the more well-to-do. Mauchline was also important for Robert Burns because it was here that his long-held interest in Scottish popular culture began to crystallize into a serious study, particularly after he met David Sillar, a collector of folk tales and poetry in the Scottish dialect.

For the next four years, until his marriage in 1788, Robert Burns' life was marked by two main themes: the poems and songs he was constantly writing and collecting and the girls he met and, all too often, became passionately interested in. There was Elizabeth Paton, for instance, a country girl who had worked in the Burns house during Willam Burnes' last illness. Her child by Robert Burns, a girl called Elizabeth, was born in May 1785; later that same summer, Burns fell in love

A statue of Robert Burns' great love, Highland Mary, was set up above the pier at Dunoon and overlooking the Firth of Clyde in 1896. Highland Mary was born on a farm called Auchnamore near Dunoon; the land the farm was on is now part of the town.

with Jean Armour, the daughter of a local mason, and they exchanged written promises to marry, which were enough in those days to be considered a binding contract. Jean Armour's parents repudiated Robert Burns, an impoverished farmer with a bad reputation, as a son-in-law and employed a lawyer, Robert Aitken of Ayr, to cut out the names from the written promises, though the papers were kept by James Armour in case of subsequent litigation. Hurt and angered by the Armours' behaviour, Burns, who by now was seriously considering emigrating to Jamaica as a way out of his many difficulties, 'repudiated' Jean.

Soon after, Burns fell in love again, this time with Mary Campbell, the 'Highland Mary' of some of his finest poetry. She was working as a dairy maid at a nearby great house, Montgomerie, where

Burns had also met 'Montgomerie's Peggy' for whom he wrote several songs. Perhaps driven by a desire to have a woman whom he could call his own, Burns exchanged bibles with Mary Campbell. The spot they chose was where the Fail Burn flowed into the River Ayr, water being considered a binding force to such a declaration. This, like the document Burns had exchanged with Jean Armour, was tantamount, in the eyes of the kirk, to a marriage contract and thus, according to the law at the time, made him a bigamist. Discretion required that their avowals should remain secret and when Mary became pregnant she returned to her family's home in Greenock, near Glasgow, having taken a tender farewell of Robert Burns in July 1786. At the end of this month, Burns had to go into hiding because James Armour had issued a writ against him. Mary Campbell died in child-birth in October 1786, a month after Jean Armour had given birth to twins, Robert and Jean, her first children by Robert Burns.

Robert Burns' anguish at the death of Mary Campbell found expression in his lovely song, *Highland Mary*:

'O, pale, pale now, those rosy lips
I aft hae kiss'd sae fondly;
And clos'd for ay, the sparkling glance
That dwalt on me sae kindly;
And mouldering now in silent dust
That heart that lo'ed me dearly!
But still within my bosum's core
Shall live my Highland Mary.'

Nothing remains of the graveyard of the old West Kirk in Greenock where Mary was buried for it was transferred to a new site in 1920 when Greenock began to develop as a great ship building centre. During the transfer, however, the body presumed to be that of Mary Campbell was found to have the body of a baby buried with it. If the woman was Mary Campbell, then the baby was Robert Burns'. He was to father fifteen children, nine of them born in 'lawful wedlock', in his life; this one, presumably, was still-born. Mary Campbell's grave is now in a new cemetery at the top of Nelson Street in Greenock.

The love of Robert Burns and Mary Campbell and their parting is commemorated by a simple stone column called Highland Mary's Monument set near the Fail Burn at Failford.

While the drama of Jean Armour's repudiation, followed by Robert Burns' pursuit by her angry father, and the tragedy of Mary Campbell had been unfolding, Robert Burns had also been trying to get some sort of order into his life. He transferred his share in the farm at Mossgiel to his brother Gilbert, made definite arrangements for his emigration to Jamaica and – most significant of all – made an agreement with a printer called John Wilson in Kilmarnock to have a selection of his poetry published.

Poems, Chiefly in the Scottish Dialect was published in Kilmarnock at the end of July 1786. It contained forty-four poems, including nine epigrams or epitaphs and four songs as well as a detailed glossary. In the collection was much of Robert Burns' finest poetry, full of romance, a love of nature and a joy in life, especially as it was lived by ordinary men and women, and a deep sense of pride in Scotland and things Scottish. Nothing like it had ever been published before in Scotland; not surprisingly, the book very quickly became a publishing sensation and Burns found himself suddenly famous. Twice in September he postponed his Jamaica voyage and at the end of October, after the death of Mary Campbell in Greenock, he abandoned it altogether.

Although Highland Mary's death left Robert Burns free to be legally joined in marriage to Jean Armour, who by now had borne him the first two of their nine children, it would be another two years before the two finally set up house together and publicly testified that they were man and wife. In the meantime, much would

TOP AND ABOVE
Two views of the house in Castle Street, Mauchline, where Robert Burns and his bride, Jean Armour, began their married life in 1788, living in just one room on the top floor of the house. The room has been kept intact and is furnished in the style of the period. Many of Robert Burns' possessions are also on display.

He in no way considered himself as abandoning either Jean Armour or Mauchline and even as he danced and sang his way through Edinburgh's high society, toured the Border country and visited the Highlands, his intentions were always to return to Mauchline.

There is much in Mauchline and the surrounding countryside, watered to the east and south by the River Ayr and the numerous burns which flow into it, to remind visitors of Robert Burns. Most recent of these reminders is the latest of the great number of statues of Robert Burns in towns all over southern Scotland, this one unveiled in Mauchline by the Princess Royal in 1995 to launch a festival planned to mark the bicentenary of Burns' death in 1796. To find most reminders of the poet in Mauchline, you must make your way to its oldest part, centred on The Cross.

In Castle Street, known as Causeway in Burns' time and which comes in to The

ABOVE
The National Burns Memorial Tower, opened in 1896, the centenary of the poet's death. A striking red sandstone building, the tower is on the A76 Dumfries-Kilmarnock road in Mauchline. It has recently been refurbished and contains an interpretation centre depicting the life of Robert Burns in Mauchline.

have happened in the life of Robert Burns himself.

In the immediate future was a trip to Edinburgh, Scotland's capital, where Robert Burns became a literary lion, fêted in the drawing rooms of the highest society of the land. Borrowing a pony, Burns set off for Edinburgh at the end of November 1786 with hope in his heart (and the passage to Jamaica, not yet sold, safely in his pocket in case of failure).

Cross at its western end, is the Burns House Museum. This was Robert Burns' first house in Mauchline after he married Jean Armour in 1788. In fact, their first home was not the whole house, just an upper room. The room has been carefully restored and furnished in the style of the time and is in the care of the Glasgow and District Burns Society. Next door is the house once occupied by Robert Burns' doctor, Dr John Mackenzie.

Mauchline Castle, nearby, is a 15th-century tower, built by the monks of Melrose Abbey. The house attached to it, still a private residence today, was the home of Robert Burns' friend and landlord, the lawyer Gavin Hamilton. Burns is thought to have married Jean Armour in a room in this house and also to have written his parody of an 'Auld Licht' sermon, *The Calf*, here.

A short walk from here brings one to Mauchline Church in Loudoun Street. In the kirkyard, four of Robert Burns' and Jean Armour's children are buried, as well as several of Burns' contemporaries who were subjects of his poems. Mauchline kirkyard was the setting for Burns' poem, *The Holy Fair*, a long, satirical look at double standards in life, bolstered by the hypocrisy Burns saw as rampant in the Church of Scotland:

'How monie hearts this day converts
O' sinners and o' lasses!
Their hearts o' stane, gin night, are gane
As saft as onie flesh is:
There's some are fou o' love divine;
There's some are fou o' brandy;
An' monie jobs that day begin,
May end in houghmagandie
Some ither day.'

Houghmagandie? That's a good dialect word for fornication, an activity much ranted against from 18th-century pulpits. Robert Burns knew all about this, having been called into Mauchline Kirk

more than once to be publicly condemned for the sin of fornication.

One of Burns' regular haunts in Mauchline was Poosie Nansie's Tavern. The setting for the Cantata *The Jolly Beggars*, in which Burns proclaimed his love of liberty, Poosie Nansie's is still a popular pub in the town.

To reach Mauchline's other sites connected with the poet, you must go north out of the town, along Kilmarnock Road. The Burns National Memorial Tower, a red sandstone tower opened in 1896 and recently refurbished, has a Tourist Information Centre on the ground floor and an 'Interpretive Centre' depicting the life of Robert Burns in Mauchline, as well as the 19th-century industrial life in Cumnock and the Doon Valley, on the floors above.

Just a mile or so from here, on the Mauchline/Tarbolton Road, is Mossgiel Farm. Still a working farm today, it may be visited, but one should inquire in advance at the Tourist Information Centre in Mauchline. Once at the farm, it does not require a great effort of imagination to 'see' the young farmer, Robbie Burns, working the land and to recall *To A Mouse: on turning her up in her nest with the plough, November 1785:*

ABOVE
Poosie Nansie's Tavern, opposite the kirkyard in Mauchline, was a popular place with Robert Burns and his friends, so popular that Burns made it the gathering place of 'the merry core O' randy, gangrel bodies' who sang the night away in his cantata *The Jolly Beggars*. Still a working pub today, Poosie Nansie's remains a popular place in the town.

LEFT
Mauchline Kirk, in the graveyard of which are buried several of Robert Burns' and Jean Armour's children. Burns included the church, and even the minister who regularly assisted at its sacraments, in his poem *The Holy Fair*.

'Wee, sleekit, cowrin, tim'rous beastie,
O, what a panic's in thy breastie!
Thou need na start awa sae hasty,
Wi' bickering brattle!
I wad be laith to rin an' chase thee,
Wi' murdering pattle!

Other places in this eastern part of Ayrshire that people following in Burns' footsteps visit include the Doon valley, today peaceful countryside but not so long ago at the centre of Ayr's industrial life, and the pretty valley down which Afton Water flows to join the River Nith at New Cumnock. A picnic area has been built round the Cairn to Robert Burns set on the banks of Afton Water just outside New Cumnock, which is the last village in Ayrshire before Dumfries and Galloway. It was Burns' delightfully romantic poem beginning 'Flow gently, sweet Afton, among thy green braes' which immortalized this quiet place.

In Robert Burns' day, Kilmarnock, nine miles to the north of Mauchline, was a comparatively small, quiet place; it began its industrialization process early in the 19th century with the establishment by a grocer called Johnny Walker of a whisky blending business. Still going strong today, the whisky bottling plant is one of the world's biggest.

Probably of interest to Robert Burns because William Wallace passed much of his youth at his uncle's farm at Riccarton, now a suburb of Kilmarnock, the town's main interest for Burns' lovers today lies in its possession of a copy of the precious first edition of the Poems. Only 612 copies were printed in 1786, selling for three shillings (fifteen new pence) each; today, the copy in Kilmarnock's Burns Monument collection of Burns' manuscripts would fetch many thousands of pounds. The monument building in Kay Park is another ornate Victorian red sandstone tower.

THE POET IN EDINBURGH

Robert Burns left Kilmarnock for Edinburgh on 27 November 1786, travelling over some of the wildest country in Ayrshire and stopping at Biggar to stay with his friends and admirers, the Prentice family. Today, the B743 to Muirkirk and the A70 crosses over the same bleak countryside, with few villages to offer the traveller a welcome. Approaching Biggar, Burns would have skirted the Tinto Hills, arid and craggy outcrops up which repentant sinners were wont to carry heavy stones. He had compensation for the journey in a very hospitable welcome which went on far into the night, leaving him with a heavy head for the rest of his journey to Edinburgh, which he reached on 29 November. Here, his friend John Richmond had invited him to share his room at Mrs Carfrae's lodgings in Baxter Close. The house was demolished long ago, but a plaque over the Lawnmarket entrance to Lady Stair's Close marks its site.

Scotland's capital in 1786 was a city in two parts. In the oldest part, around what is now called the Royal Mile between the Castle and the royal palace of Holyrood, grandeur and squalor lived side by side. The streets were either cobbled or unpaved and noble houses abutted on the slums of the poor as well as on inns, taverns and brothels. Animals of all kinds were permitted to wander unchecked, fouling the streets; at night, despite threats of heavy fines, the slops from basins and chamberpots were still occasionally emptied out of windows with cries of 'Gardy loo', a Scottish version of 'Gardez l'eau'. Boswell and Dr Johnson had complained of this habit some years earlier during their visit to Edinburgh and the Highlands.

The other part of Edinburgh, the New Town, was something quite different. By the time Robert Burns arrived in the city the layout of the New Town, a wonderfully imaginative town planning scheme dreamed up by George Drummond, Lord Provost of Edinburgh five times between 1725 and 1764, was largely completed and elegant Georgian buildings were going up in the squares and along the terraces and streets on land once known as Barefoot's Parks on the far side of the Nor' Loch.

Today, this part of Edinburgh is dominated by two single-sided terraces – Princes Street, facing south towards the Castle and High Street, and Queen Street, facing towards the Firth of Forth – with George Street between them, providing a splendid central thoroughfare linking St Andrew's Square in the east and Charlotte Square (originally called St George's Square) with buildings designed by the great Robert Adam in 1791 in the west. The fine church of St Andrew in George Street had been completed in the year before Robert Burns arrived in Edinburgh, though its tall, thin spire was not added until 1789.

Although he began his Edinburgh life in the very heart of old Edinburgh, Burns also lived in the New Town, at No. 2 St James's Square, where he was given a room by the owner, William Cruikshank, a Classical Master at the Edinburgh High School. He came here after his tours of the Borders and Highlands in 1787 and spent much of his time working on the second

volume of *Scots Musical Museum*, the first volume of which came out in May 1787. This publication, which eventually ran to four volumes published between 1787 and 1792, was the brainchild of an Edinburgh engraver, James Johnson; most of the textual work in it was produced by Robert Burns, who became its literary editor in fact, if not in name and included many of his own songs as well as those his researches discovered. Like the house in Baxter Close, No. 2 St James's Square has gone, demolished along with the rest of the square in the 1960s to make way for a shopping centre, the St James' Centre.

Described by the Scottish writer Malcolm Macdonald as a place 'of undeniable convenience and quite remarkable hideousness, like a prefabricated concrete lavatory built for a race of giants', the St James' Centre is unlikely to rouse in the minds of Burns' admirers any ghostly reminders of the poet's residence in this part of the city. Not far from here, however, there is a very real reminder of Burns in the form of Edinburgh's Monument to

Robert Burns. This circular monument, designed in the style of a Greek temple by Thomas Hamilton, is at the western end of Regent Terrace, where it joins Regent Road in the Eastern New Town, planned and built in the early 19th century. The Monument to Robert Burns was unveiled in 1830.

For Robert Burns, newly arrived in Edinburgh, his surroundings were probably a matter of indifference. He was in Edinburgh to try to build on the success of the Kilmarnock edition of his poems and on his sudden fame. He was planning a second edition of his poems and he had introductions to influential people in Edinburgh.

From the time of his arrival, armed with a letter of introduction to the Earl of Glencairn, he was lionized by the cultured society of the capital. It was a time when the idea of the simplicity and purity of natural man, as proposed by the Genevan philosopher Jean Jacques Rousseau, was much in vogue. Burns was admired as a prototype, the natural man, a ploughman capable of sensibility and art. The Earl of Glencairn introduced him to Edinburgh salon society and he soon became much sought-after, invited as a guest into the

A pipe band leads the parade at the start of the Edinburgh Festival Cavalcade; behind, the Robert Burns Monument in Regent Road dominates the skyline. Like the Burns Monument in Alloway, this one is in the rather inappropriate style of a Grecian temple. The architect was Thomas Hamilton, who designed other buildings in this part of Edinburgh's New Town, including the Royal High School, which may one day house a Scottish Assembly should current proposals to return a measure of self-rule to Scotland *bear fruit.*

houses of the rich and powerful including the Earl himself and the 4th Duke of Gordon, whose wife, Jane, Duchess of Gordon, was an unconventional beauty who numbered among her friends the Prime Minister William Pitt and Henry Dundas, who had been Lord Advocate of Scotland and was at this time President of the Board of Trade and a close associate of Pitt.

With such connections Burns was accepted by everyone, including the writer Henry Mackenzie, whose novel *The Man of Feeling* was cherished by Burns as one of his favourite books and who himself praised Burns' Kilmarnock poems in the literary periodical, *The Lounger*, and the bookseller William Creech, who would later become Lord Provost of Edinburgh; such men set the fashion in Edinburgh's cultured society. It was William Creech who arranged the publication of the Edinburgh edition of Burns' poems in April 1787, though Burns paid the printer and binder himself. The edition eventually sold a handsome 3,000 copies, at a price of five shillings to subscribers and six shillings to the public. It was to William

Creech that Burns sold the copyright in his poems for 100 guineas a month after their publication in Edinburgh.

Through all the adulation – indeed in response to it – Burns continued to write poetry. One poem, *Address to Edinburgh*, began 'Edina! Scotia's darling seat!'; another was the immortal *Address to a Haggis*.

Plans for the Edinburgh edition of Burns' poems were soon under way, though there had to be a certain amount of judicious deleting. Some works that might offend the authorities and the Kirk were left out. Though acceptable in society, Burns' coarse and libidinous side was beginning to be talked about and he had to be discreet. Besides, the book was to be sponsored by the Caledonian Hunt, a body that represented Edinburgh society with all its prejudices.

The Edinburgh edition of Burns' poems was much larger than the Kilmarnock one, with twenty-two more poems, including such now world-famous pieces as *Address to a Haggis, Death and Dr. Hornbook, The Brigs of Ayr, John Barleycorn,* which was in praise of whisky, and *Green Grow the Rashes.* There was for several generations a tradition current in Latin America that it was this last song which gave the word 'gringo', meaning an English-speaking newcomer, to the language, apparently because so many British people, especially Scots, in Latin America had sung it.

Among poems left out of the Edinburgh edition were those satirical pieces which derided the Kirk for its hypocrisy and narrow-mindedness, such as *The Holy Fair,* and various private pieces from his Commonplace Book, deemed unpublishable because of their vulgarity. One such was a bawdy song called *My Girl She's Airy,* addressed to a girl called Lizzie Paton, who had helped out at Lochlea when William Burnes had been so ill:

*'Her slender neck, her handsome waist
Her hair well buckl'd, her stays well lac'd,
Her taper-white leg, with an et and a, c
For her a, b,e,d, and her c,u,n,t,
And Oh, for the joys of a long winter
night!!!'*

During his first stay in Edinburgh Burns did little travelling outside the city for he was busy making useful contacts. He made a point of joining many clubs and societies, many of them based in inns and taverns, where men gathered. Although he had been well received in society, he remained something of a curiosity and his life took on a certain duplicity; while he mingled with the rich and powerful, his own inclinations took him into many of the inns and clubs of Edinburgh, such as Johnnie Dowie's in Liberton's Wynd, the Anchor-Close tavern in the High Street, where a drinking club called the Crochallan Fencibles met, and the White Hart Inn which still stands on the north side of Grassmarket.

It was not just that the earthy, bawdy side of Edinburgh life naturally appealed to Burns; there was also the fact that it was among ordinary folk that he was most likely to find the tunes and traditional songs which had become a consuming interest, leading him to the grassroots of Scottish culture, which, even at this time, was beginning to disappear. It was this interest as much as a desire to become better known that led him to consider tours of Scotland during which he could talk to people, lecture, and travel to every corner where he might find shreds of a culture which had been passed on orally for generations.

For the present-day visitor following in Burns' footsteps in the capital city, there is no better place to start than Edinburgh Castle, set on the highest point of a splendidly defensible volcanic rock along which stretches the oldest and most historic part of Edinburgh. The Castle has been a defensive place since the time of the Picts and Scots. One of its great glories today is the lovely St Margaret's Chapel, built by Malcolm Canmore's saintly wife, Queen Margaret. The chapel is believed to have been built in 1076, but was neglected for centuries and only restored in the mid-19th century. The castle was also the birthplace of Mary, Queen of Scots' son, James, who, as James VI of Scotland, was to unite the thrones of Scotland and England when he became James I of England on the death of Queen Elizabeth I.

The entrance to the castle is by the wide Castle Esplanade on which the world-famous and colourful Military Tattoo takes place during the annual Edinburgh International Festival. Around the Esplanade are memorial plaques to the fallen of many Scottish regiments as well as, at the small bronze Witches' Well, a reminder that more than 300 witches were burned here, the last one in 1722.

From the Esplanade, visitors cross a moat to the Castle gateway, flanked by statues of the Scottish heroes Robert the Bruce and Sir William Wallace; the statues are modern, so Robert Burns would not have known these monuments to his

The White Hart Inn, on the north side of Grassmarket. This may have been one of the first inns Robert Burns visited when he reached Edinburgh, for the great open space of Grassmarket, for centuries the city's hay and agricultural market and the site of many public executions, was the point at which Burns arrived in the city in 1786. Once settled in Edinburgh, Burns spent numerous convivial evenings in the White Hart Inn.

favourite Scottish heroes.

At the centre of the castle complex is Crown Square, around which are to be found the very moving Scottish National War Memorial, the Crown Room, Queen Mary's Apartments, where James V1 was born, the old Parliament or Banqueting Hall and the Scottish United Services Museum, one of the 'treasures' of which is the enormous cannon Mons Meg.

From Edinburgh Castle an historic line of streets, known as the Royal Mile, descends all the way down the spine of the rock east to Holyrood Palace. The streets, in order from the Castle end, are Castle Hill, Lawnmarket, High Street and Canongate. Until the 18th-century development of the New Towns across the Nor' Loch this was where the life of Edinburgh was lived, and it was the Edinburgh which Burns knew best for he

had come into the city on its south side at the Grassmarket, once a place of execution as well as a market, and still a fairly rough area: the grave robbers, Burke and Hare, were most active in the alleys of Grassmarket early in the 19th century, murdering drunks and tramps to keep full the dissecting table of the anatomist, Robert Knox.

Descending the Royal Mile one of the first place of interest one encounters, at the top of the steps descending to the Grassmarket, is Cannonball House with what is said to be a cannonball intended for Bonnie Prince Charlie still embedded in its wall. On the opposite side of the Royal Mile is the Outlook Tower, a viewpoint for Edinburgh since the 17th century, but only really popular since 1850 when its camera obscura was installed.

From this point, Castle Hill becomes

Small streets, alleyways and wynds lead off the Royal Mile into courts and closes of great age. Although many of the houses in these closes have gone, including the one in Baxter Close where Burns stayed, many more have been refurbished and stylishly restored. A fine example of these is this building in Milne's Court.

RIGHT
Canongate Kirk dates from the last year of James VII and II's reign. It was built to provide a place of worship for the parishioners of the Chapel Royal in Holyrood, whom the king had ejected.

the Lawnmarket, so named because it was once a market for the sale of flax and linen. This was a very respectable part of Edinburgh in the late 18th century, lived in by such well-known people as David Hume and James Boswell, both of whom had a flat in James Court; Gladstone's Land in Lawnmarket is a typical Edinburgh tenement; now owned by the National Trust for Scotland, it is furnished in 17th-century style. Not too far away, in Brodie's Close, lived the not-so-respectable Deacon Brodie, a respected councillor by day but thief by night, on whom Robert Louis Stevenson based his story of Dr Jekyll and Mr Hyde. Deacon Brodie was finally caught trying to rob a local Excise Office and was hanged in 1788.

In Lady Stair's Close, a short distance from Gladstone's Land, is Lady Stair's House, another fine example of 17th-century domestic architecture. Today the building houses the Writers' Museum, with collections of material about the lives and works of Robert Burns, Walter Scott and Robert Louis Stevenson.

Lawnmarket comes to an end in an area of important buildings including Parliament House, St Giles' Cathedral, and the City Chambers. Parliament House dates from the 17th century but was given a new Italian-style façade in the 19th century. This was the meeting place of the Scottish parliament until 1707 when the Act of Union made it unnecessary.

St Giles' Cathedral, the High Kirk of Scotland, was built during the 15th century on the foundation of a previous Norman Church. It suffered considerable damage during the Reformation, when its many altars and the statue of St Giles were thrown into the Nor' Loch. The interior of the building today features a large number of commemorative memorials to Scottish regiments and also contains the chapel of the Most Ancient and Most Noble Order of the Thistle, Scotland's

highest order of chivalry, founded in 1687 by James VII and II.

For followers of Robbie Burns, the most important item of interest in St Giles' is the great West Window, which is dedicated to the poet. The window was commissioned as recently as 1985, and even then, nearly 200 years after his death, the event caused considerable controversy for many people felt that such a womanizer and hardened drinker was an unsuitable candidate for the honour, be he never so much the nation's bard. It is a matter on which the great Calvinist reformer John Knox would have had plenty to say; his house is only just down the street, in the High Street section of the Royal Mile.

Just below John Knox House was Netherbow Port, the old lower gate into the city; from here, the Royal Mile becomes Canongate, so called because the canons of the old Abbey of Holyrood lived here. Before walking on down Canongate to the Palace of Holyrood, scene of so many stirring events in Scotland's history, Burns' admirers may find another trace of the poet in Canongate Church, for among the notable Scots buried in the Canongate kirkyard is the greatly under-valued poet, Robert Fergusson, who died in Edinburgh's Mad House just a year after publishing his *Poems* in 1773. Robert Burns knew Fergusson's work well, writing of him that he was

My elder brother in misfortune
By far my elder brother in the Muse.

He was distressed to discover, when he came to Edinburgh, that Fergusson's grave was unmarked. The headstone on the grave today was commissioned and paid for by Burns, whose words are inscribed on it.

At the eastern end of the Royal Mile is the Palace of Holyroodhouse, or Holyrood Palace, still the official residence of the sovereign in Scotland. Before the palace became a royal residence it was a guest house for the Abbey of Holyrood, founded, like the four great abbeys of the Borders, by King David I. James IV made the guest house his palace, and Mary, Queen of Scots came to live here on her return from France after the death of her husband, the Dauphin of France. Charles II had the palace rebuilt in the French style and this was the building which Bonnie Prince Charlie made his headquarters during the heady early days of the Rebellion of 1745. Among its finest rooms are the Charles II State Apartments, though that king never stayed in them, the Picture Gallery and the Historical Apartments, which are what remains of the old palace. Among the rooms here is the apartment in which Mary, Queen of Scots witnessed the murder of her secretary, David Rizzio, by followers of her husband, Lord Darnley.

The present-day visitor to Edinburgh is as likely to spend as much time in Princes Street and the streets beyond as on the Royal Mile, for these make up the modern centre of Edinburgh, with many shops, restaurants, museums and other entertainments. To the west of this lively area rises Calton Hill, a viewpoint offering a sweeping panorama taking in the Castle rock, the Georgian New Towns and several monuments.

When Burns arrived in Edinburgh this was still very much a rural area and a pleasant place for walks, rivalled only by the heights behind Holyrood Park and the volcanic hills known as Arthur's Seat. The Edinburgh of Burns' day was a relatively small place with a close-knit society. No doubt, Burns escaped now and again into the surrounding countryside. Little of this remains, of course, for the industrial developments of the 19th century filled the riverside with warehouses and shipyards. Upriver, Burns might have visited Linlithgow and its royal palace and Falkirk, now in the midst of industrial

development. To the south, then as now, was the unspoilt sweep of the Pentland Hills, with the Borders beyond them to the south.

For Burns, the Borders soon began to hold such attractions that it was not long before he was planning a tour of the region. He would leave Edinburgh and go searching for songs, poetry and the speech of ordinary Scots folk among the historic towns of Scotland's most southerly land.

PAGES 42-43
Some of the finest views of Edinburgh are from Calton Hill. Dominating the horizon in this photograph is the great bulk of Edinburgh Castle.

BURNS IN THE BORDER COUNTRY

The lovely valley of the Tweed, one of the great rivers of the Border region, which flows east to reach the sea at Berwick-upon-Tweed, in England. Burns visited many of the historic towns along the river, including Kelso, Melrose and Dryburgh.

After some months in Edinburgh, Burns began to feel the need to get away for a time and began making plans to tour the Border country. This was to be as much an exploration of the folk culture, especially the songs and language, of the region as a tour of the old towns and historic sites, and was widely discussed with friends before he left the capital early in May 1787.

Among the many admirers whom Robert Burns had acquired in Edinburgh one who became a close friend was Mrs

Frances Dunlop of Dunlop, a mature widow who had been so impressed by her first reading of *The Cotter's Saturday Night* that she had immediately bought several copies of Burns' poetry for giving to friends, including the economist Adam Smith. Burns, always flattered by unstinted admiration, soon developed a platonic relationship with Mrs Dunlop, who became his confidante in the city. She was one of the first to know of Burns' plans for an extended tour of the Borders.

'I have no greater, no dearer aim than

... to make leisurely pilgrimages through Caledonia ... ' he had written to her; '... to sit on the fields of her battles; to wander on the romantic banks of her rivers; and to muse by the stately tower or venerable ruins, once the honoured abode of her heroes.' In fact, as his own journal of his Border tours indicates, Burns usually had more to say about the people he met than the places he saw, with many of his comments on places being quite laconic. He showed more interest in the quality of the farmland than he did in the many historic sites of battles that are dotted across the Border country: he must have passed very close to the site of the Battle of Flodden, for instance, but there is no mention of it in his journal. He also seems to have ignored, or failed to notice, the old tradition of ballad writing, which had been a feature of life in the monasteries attached to the great abbeys at Jedburgh, Melrose, Dryburgh and Kelso, all of which he visited. For Robert Burns, song and the speech of the people were the things that mattered.

Burns' romantic passion for all things Scottish was very real, but there was also a deal of self-interest in his plans, for he wanted to become more widely known as a poet and create a more comfortable life for himself than that of a farmer. Not that farming was to be abandoned. One object of his Borders tour was to inspect a farm near Dumfries the lease of which had been offered him by an admirer, a businessman and banker called Patrick Miller who had recently bought an estate at Dalswinton, on the River Nith.

Robert Burns' tour of the Border country lasted some five weeks, turning into a sort of triumphant poet's progress as it went on, and it is very easy for present-day admirers to follow in his footsteps because his journal was kept up in detail. He used as his main base the home of his travelling companion for the first weeks of the trip, a young and carefree law student

called Robert Ainslie, whose family lived at Berrywell, near Duns, on the southern edge of the Lammermuir Hills. From this house, Burns did three laps, as it were, of the Borders, all three of which took him over the border into England.

Burns and Robert Ainslie rode out from Edinburgh on 5 May 1787, Burns riding his newly acquired mare Jenny Geddes, named after the Edinburgh woman famous for having thrown her stool at the Bishop of Edinburgh in St Giles' Cathedral in 1637, in protest at having the Book of Common Prayer foisted on the Church in Scotland. The small party arrived at Berrywell that evening. The ride over the Lammermuir hills by way of Haddington, Gifford and Longformacus, was easy and comfortable, though, because of the time of year, 'miserably dreary, but at times very picturesque', for the hills are low and undulating with green farmlands and moors where long ago powerful reivers extracted payments from farmers in exchange for 'protection' against cattle rustlers. Later, this became sheep-raising country. Today, the Lammermuir Hills, watered by many rivers and streams which have carved out pretty valleys, make good walking country for ramblers with plenty to interest them,

Jedburgh, historically the most interesting of the Border towns, was thought by Burns to be 'charming and romantic'. Much of the romance of Jedburgh lies in its connections with Mary, Queen of Scots who stayed in the town in 1566 in a house which remains one of its main tourist attractions.

The fine stone bridge over the Tweed at Coldstream, which Robert Burns and his friend Robert Ainslie used to cross into England in May 1787, was built by an English engineer, John Smeaton, in 1766. It replaced the ford which had been the river's crossing place at this point for centuries.

for the area is dotted with prehistoric remains, including hill forts and brochs, and the ruins of priories and castles of more recent times.

Duns, a few miles inland from the North Sea coast town of Eyemouth and even nearer to the historic Border crossing at Coldstream on the Tweed, is a village built on the lower slopes of Duns Laws. On the summit of this hill a stone commemorates the gathering of Leslie's army of Covenanters opposed to Charles I's efforts to impose a new prayer book in 1639. The present village of Duns dates only from the late 16th century, the original village having been destroyed by the English in 1545. Since then Duns has been a quiet market town, its only disagreement with the English being the claim to be the birthplace of Duns Scotius, the medieval philosopher who is also claimed as a local

son by both Northumberland and County Down in Northern Ireland. In the 20th century, some fame has come to Duns as the birthplace of the World Motor Racing Champion, Jim Clark.

Burns and Ainslie were in Duns on a Sunday, and so went to church. The following day, they rode south to Coldstream and crossed the Tweed into England. 'Tweed was clear and majestic – fine bridge,' Burns noted in his journal.

The bridge over the Tweed at Coldstream is indeed a fine structure, built in 1766 by the English engineer John Smeaton who was also responsible for the Eddystone lighthouse and the Forth and Clyde Canal. In earlier centuries, armies of both Scots and English had had to ford the river at Coldstream. Burns' hero Robert the Bruce used the ford at Coldstream on several occasions when he was fighting Edward II of England. In 1513 this was the way James IV and his army went into England, to be met just three miles south of the Border by an English army at Flodden Field near Branxton. Weighed down in the mud by their heavy armour, James IV, his son, many nobles and nearly 9000 soldiers were killed.

Coldstream is a small town, built above a bend of the River Tweed with wooded hills making a picturesque setting for its stone houses. This was a scene of many skirmishes between Scots and English. Nearby on the south bank of the Tweed are the ruins of Wark Castle, once defended for England by the Countess of Salisbury against the Scottish king David II. Legend has it that when Edward III visited the castle he became enamoured of the Countess and while dancing with her picked up her garter which had fallen off, returning it to her with the now famous comment 'Honi soit qui mal y pense' which are the words round the badge of the Order of the Garter, England's premier order of chivalry.

At the time of the Restoration of Charles II, Coldstream gave its name to one of the most famous regiments in the British Army, the Coldstream Guards, which was raised by General Monk in the town before he headed south to play a major part in the Restoration. The regiment has its own museum in the town.

West of Coldstream lie the estates of The Hirsel, seat of the Douglas Home family, an ancient Border family whose most famous member was Sir Alec Douglas Home, the statesman who was both Foreign Secretary and Prime Minister of Britain.

Robert Burns' first visit to England was just a day trip. He slept at Coldstream and the next day began a tour which would take him to places with some of the most famous names in the Borders before ending the first lap of his trip back at Berrywell. Kelso and nearby Roxburgh Castle, Jedburgh, Dryburgh, Melrose, Selkirk and the Ettrick valley, including Traquair House, said to be the oldest continuously inhabited house in Scotland, were all visited and noted in the journal at this time.

Kelso lies nine miles upstream of Coldstream on the Tweed. It is as handsome a town today as it was when Burns breakfasted there and visited the ruins of nearby Roxburgh Castle. Kelso has a very fine central square, with Georgian houses lining the vast cobbled space which at one time resounded to the rattle of carriage wheels and the stamp of soldiers' boots. A high point in its colourful past was when the Old Pretender was proclaimed James VIII at a gathering of the clans. A sadder moment was when Bonnie Prince Charlie's retreating army assembled there during their march back north to eventual defeat at Culloden.

The gaunt remains of the Abbey are a reminder of the historic importance of the Border towns and of the part that religious communities played in administering the social and economic life of the country. The Abbey was destroyed by besieging English in 1545, when its defenders, which

Burns probably breakfasted near Kelso's 18th-century Town Hall when he arrived early in the morning from Coldstream.The Town Hall, from whose tower the curfew is still rung during the Civic Week in July, is the main building in Kelso's cobbled Market Square.

included its few remaining monks, were slaughtered.

Over the Tweed, crossed here by John Rennie's handsome five-arched bridge of 1803, which he used as model for Waterloo Bridge in London, lies a green and wooded countryside in the midst of which are the few remains of Roxburgh Castle. This was once the most powerful castle in the Borders and was surrounded by a large town. The remains of stone walls and gateways now overgrown with trees and undergrowth leave a haunting impression.

Back on the Kelso side of the river valley can be glimpsed a castle which stands out in pristine splendour among the trees of its parkland. This is Floors Castle, the seat of the dukes of Roxburgh. It was built by William Adam in the 18th century and refurbished to its present appearance in the 19th century, providing visitors with a glimpse of the elegant and gracious life of Scottish nobility in these more peaceful times. In the grounds of Floors is a yew tree which all the guide books tell us marks the spot where James II of Scotland was standing during his seige of Roxburgh, then in the hands of the English, when a cannon exploded and killed him. Burns, visiting what was then Roxburgh Palace, noted in his diary that he was shown a holly bush, 'growing where James II was accidentally killed by the bursting of a cannon'.

Though Burns is remembered today for his association with this historic and fascinating part of the Borders, which he visited with great interest, gathering material for the *Scots Musical Museum* as he went, the poetic and literary associations of the landscape are much more closely connected with Sir Walter Scott. He, like Burns, was greatly inspired by grassroots Scottish culture, expressing it first in his poetry, such as *The Lay of the Last Minstrel*, with its references to Melrose Abbey and the Eildon Hills, then in his Waverley novels. While Burns was travelling in the Tweed valley, Scott was still a very young man in Edinburgh but the modern traveller can enjoy the connection of both Burns and Scott with the Borders as their paths cross at many places.

Melrose was one such. Still a small town, its importance lies in its possession of the ruins of one of the four great abbeys built in the Borders in the 12th century. Melrose Abbey, as romantic a collection of ruins in Burns' time as it is today, was founded by David I for Cistercian monks from Rielvaux in Yorkshire. It suffered considerably from the passage of English armies, Robert the Bruce, whose heart is said to be buried near the high altar, restoring it in 1326 after its first brush with the English. It was finally destroyed by Hertford in 1545.

Enough remains of the Abbey to give a good idea of the magnificence of the original building, especially in the main part of the church and tower where much of the masonry remains. In this part of the church are the tombs of several members of the Douglas family, of Alexander II and of that semi-legendary character Michael Scot the Wizard who, kidnapped by fairies when a child, became a magician able to weave spells with which he could even outwit the Devil.

Between Melrose and Kelso lies countryside closely associated with Sir Walter Scott. On the B6397 is Smailholm Tower, a fine example of a Border peel tower which took a strong hold over Scott's imagination when he came here as a boy.

The isolated situation of the tower, which stands on a mound by a small loch, creates a memorable scene. Visitors to Smailholm often include nearby Mellerstain House on their tour. Begun by William Adam and completed by his son Robert, this is one of the finest and most elegantly detailed of all 18th-century Scottish mansions. The ceilings and walls are rich in Robert Adam decorative fea-

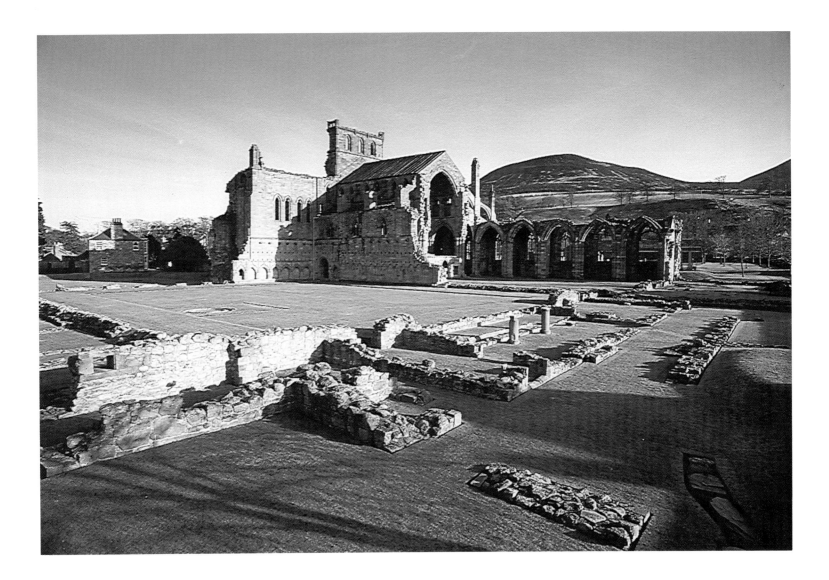

tures, the furniture is by such famous designers as Sheraton and Hepplewhite and there is a collection of fine paintings by old Masters including Veronese, Gainsborough and the Scot Allan Ramsay.

After his death in 1832, Scott was buried at Dryburgh Abbey, another of the Border country's great abbeys, founded in the 12th century by Hugh de Morville, Constable of Scotland. The abbey's setting on the river Tweed amid trees is beautiful and there are pleasant walks along the river and to the nearby village of Newton St Boswell.

Although Burns saw Dryburgh Abbey, he would not have visited Sir Walter Scott's famous house, Abbotsford, near Melrose. Scott bought the simple farmhouse which he turned into Abbotsford in 1811 and spent twenty

years and a great deal of money transforming it into the splendidly turreted Gothic pile one sees today. There is a Burns connection, however, for among the contents of the extraordinary museum Scott collected at Abbotsford is – appropriately enough – one of Burns' drinking cups.

One of the objectives of Burns' tour of the Borders was to collect traditional airs and this is what drew him to Jedburgh, a town with many historic connections. Burns took a room at 27 Canongate, in a house now demolished, and saw enough of the town, attractively set on a hill above Jed Water, to think it 'charming and romantic.'

The well-read Burns would certainly have known that Jedburgh's history was long and turbulent. The Romans had been here for several generations; there had

Melrose Abbey, lying between the Tweed and the Eildon Hills, was one of the four great abbeys built in the Borders during the reign of David I. Largely destroyed by the English Earl of Hertford during Henry VIII's 'rough wooing' of Mary, Queen of Scots, its magnificent ruins are an impressive reminder of its former power and importance.

been a Christian presence from at least the 9th century, reaching a high point in the 12th century with the founding of another of David I's abbeys by Augustinian monks from France; and, of course, there had been cross-Border fighting for centuries. Even royal connections with the town had been, if not charming, then certainly romantic.

Alexander III was married in Jedburgh Abbey in 1285, with the wedding feast in Jedburgh Castle disturbed by the appearance of a ghostly figure prophesying doom for both king and country; a year later, the king was dead and the country in turmoil. Mary, Queen of Scots stayed in Jedburgh in 1566; while here, she heard that her lover, the Earl of Bothwell, was lying wounded in Hermitage Castle after a Border skirmish and impetuously rode the twenty miles across country beyond Hawick to Hermitage to see him, returning the same day to Jedburgh. While the house in which Mary stayed in Jedburgh is one of the attractions of the town for modern visitors, the most impressive building remains the ruined red sandstone abbey. The castle which once crowned the hill was deliberately destroyed by the Scots to keep it out of English hands; 400 years later, the town jail was built on what was left of its foundations.

Burns lingered longer than he had intended at Jedburgh because a young woman called Isabella Lindsay took his fancy; today, visitors linger because of the beauty of the wooded hills which provide many opportunities for walks.

After Jedburgh and his peregrinations round the towns of the Tweed valley, Burns turned north to Selkirk and the Ettrick valley. Burns was continuing to collect songs and to write poetry of his own during his tour; while staying at the Old Forest Inn in Selkirk he found time to write about business to his publisher William Creech, and also to send him a copy of the poem called *Willie's Awa'*

which he had just written deploring Creech's absence in London on business:

'Auld chuckie REEKIE'S [Dear old
Edinburgh is] sair distrest
Down droops her ance weel-burnishe'd crest
Nae joy her bonie buskit [beautifully
dressed] nest
Can yield ava [at all];
Her darling bird that she lo'es best,
Willie's awa ....'

Like many buildings associated with Robbie Burns, the Old Forest Inn in Selkirk is long gone; a plaque marking its site has been erected in the road approaching the west side of the Market Place.

Selkirk is in an attractive setting on a hillside above Ettrick Water, a fine salmon and trout stream which rises in the high country west of the Ettrick Forest and flows down a fine vale to join the Tweed two miles beyond Selkirk. William Wallace was proclaimed Guardian of Scotland in the town at the end of the 13th century; over a century later, much of Selkirk was burned by the victorious English after the Battle of Flodden.

Selkirk makes a good base for visitors wanting to explore this part of the Borders region, dominated by the vast area of the Ettrick Forest, which was once a royal hunting ground and also a place of refuge for men like William Wallace and Robert the Bruce as well as for outlaws and fugitives from royal justice.

Most of the forest which once covered the land has gone, with moorland being the main feature of the landscape. Two fine rivers, the Ettrick and the Yarrow, flow through lovely wooded vales, both of them well supplied with fine houses. In the Ettrick valley is Oakwood Tower, supposedly the home of Michael Scot the Wizard, and in the Yarrow valley is the imposing mansion, Bowhill, a seat of the dukes of Buccleuch. The house stands amid dense woods above the river and is well fur-

Selkirk's Market Place in spring. Selkirk's setting above Ettrick Water was as attractive in Burns' time as today, though Burns felt a particular interest in the town because his hero, William Wallace, had been declared Guardian of Scotland here. Much later, Sir Walter Scott was county sheriff of Selkirk for many years, and it is his statue which now stands in Market Square, rather than than of the great Scottish patriot.

nished in the French style. There is a fine collection of paintings including works by Leonardo da Vinci, Claude, Gainsborough and Raeburn.

A place where Burns was received hospitably was Innerleithen, on the Tweed about 15 miles upstream from Selkirk. At Innerleithen, he stayed at an inn in what was then called Piccadilly, and is now the High Street; the inn was demolished in the 1860s, but a plaque on a wall in the High Street marks its site.

In his journal, Burns noted that Traquair House, said to be the oldest inhabited house in Scotland, was in the vicinity. Among the many famous people received there had been several Scottish and English monarchs, including William the Lion and Mary, Queen of Scots, as well as Bonnie Prince Charlie. The present house was built in the 17th century round the ancient peel tower and includes such delights as a priests' hideaway and secret stairway. In the same sentence as his note on Traquair, Burns also remarked on having seen 'Elibanks and Elibraes, so famous in baudy song today', on the other side of the Tweed. Almost

certainly, the latter had more significance for him than the great house. He included the old song, though he was never satisfied with his 'touching-up' of the text, in Merry Muses of Caledonia, a 'collection of favourite Scots Songs, Ancient and Modern' gathered together for his friends in an Edinburgh drinking club, the Crochallan Fencibles.

From the Ettrick valley, Burns returned to Berrywell before undertaking the second lap of his Borders tour, which took him to the east coast of the region and into England again. It is possible that the patriotic Burns felt that in visiting Berwick-upon-Tweed he was not really leaving Scotland behind, for Berwick had been a Scottish town for centuries. During the long period of the Border conflicts, Berwick had changed hands no fewer than thirteen times before Richard Duke of Gloucester, later Richard III, finally took the town for England in 1482.

Its position meant that Berwick-upon-Tweed became one of the most heavily fortified towns on the Border; even Queen Elizabeth I, early in her reign, had felt it necessary to strengthen Berwick's fortifi-

cations. By the time Burns came to visit the town its impressive sea walls had become a place for promenading. While walking along them, Burns was pleased to be recognized by Lord Errol, who admired his poetry. Burns, it seems, was less pleased with Berwick, which he called 'an idle town but rudely picturesque'. There is a story that he disliked the place enough to scratch a verse on a pane of glass in his lodging which ran 'Berwick is a dirty place. Has a church without a steeple. A midden stands at every door, And a damned deceitful people.' Another version of the verse goes 'Berwick is an ancient town. A church without a steeple. A pretty girl at every door, And very generous people'.

The coast north of Berwick seemed more to Burns' liking. At Eyemouth, a small fishing port, Burns even went for a sail, probably the first time he had been on the sea. Today, Eyemouth becomes a seaside resort during the summer months, holding fishing competitions and marine galas to entertain visitors.

The most impressive part of this stretch of the coast is St Abb's Head, a promontory whose high cliffs pounded by the sea provides a continuous and enthralling spectacle. Many varieties of seabirds come here every year, either during migration or to nest and rear young.

While he was in Eyemouth, Burns was made a royal arch-Mason of the Masonic Lodge of St Ebbe's, being admitted *gratis*; his companion Ainslie had to pay a guinea for his subscription. Burns described the Lodge's eldest brother, Mr William Grieves, as 'a joyous, warm-hearted, jolly, clever fellow – takes a hearty glass and sings a good song'.

Slightly inland from the coast here is the village of Coldingham, which Burns stopped at on his way to Dunbar (passing through 'the most glorious corn country I ever saw'). Coldingham is a summer resort today but was once the site of a

Priory founded in 1098 by King Edgar of Northumbria to replace a 7th-century nunnery on St Abb's Head which had been destroyed by Norsemen. The Priory suffered a similar fate at the hands of the English and was virtually demolished by Cromwell, though some remains are incorporated in Coldingham's parish church. Relics of the time when this part of the Borders was a battlefield between Scots and English are visible at Fast Castle, the gaunt ruins of a former stronghold of the Homes, which stands on a rocky eminence by the sea four miles north of Coldingham.

Burns went as far north along this coast as Dunbar, where he dined with the Provost and his wife. Another town which had seen more than its fair share of stirring events, including giving refuge to Mary, Queen of Scots and her husband Lord Darnley after the murder of David Rizzio, Dunbar had become by Burns' time a quiet place which he noted in his journal as a 'neat little town'. Its once mighty castle was destroyed by Scotland's Regent, Moray, after Mary, Queen of Scots' army had been defeated at Carberry Hill. Oliver Cromwell completed the castle's destruction by using its stones to rebuild the harbour, which is today the town's most interesting and attractive area.

The final lap of Burns' Borders tour took him from Berrywell, where he had had to bid farewell to his delightful travelling companion, Robert Ainslie, as far over the Border as Newcastle, then across to Carlisle. From here, he went back over the Border into Scotland and up beyond Dumfries to look at Patrick Miller's Dalswinton property, before returning home to the family farm at Mossgiel.

Burns made his way to Newcastle on England's north-east coast via Wooler, on the moors at the eastern end of the Cheviot Hills, arriving at Alnwick, a town dominated by the great castle of the Percy family headed by the Duke of Northumberland, on 27 May. Alnwick

Castle, when Burns visited it, had been going through a great period of restoration which would last until well into the 19th century and Burns, shown round by one of the Duke's agents, thought the castle 'furnished in a most princely manner'.

The Newcastle which Burns reached on 29 May, by way of Warkworth and Morpeth, was not yet the great shipping and coal exporting port that it would become in the 19th century, though at this time it had a good trade in wool and cloth. Burns' stay in the town was brief, and he was soon off westwards across northern England, making for Carlisle, which he reached on 31 May, by way of Hexham, Wardrew and Longtoun, a market town on the River Esk where, by good luck, it was a hiring day. 'I am uncommonly happy to see so many young folks enjoying life,' he noted in his journal.

Once again, Burns' stay in historic Carlisle was brief. Even so, he had time to note in his journal that he had a 'strange romantic adventure' with a girl who wanted to take him over the Border to Gretna Green, a place notorious for the instant marriages which could be obtained there. Burns wrote that since he was not such a 'gull' as she thought him he gave her a 'brush of caressing and a bottle of cyder' but promised her nothing.

In Carlisle he was shown round his 'good friend' Mr Mitchell's printing works, and thought it worth noting that the works employed four or five hundred people, including many women and children. Once again, we can record where Burns stayed in Carlisle, the Malt Shovel Inn in Rickergate, only to note that the inn was demolished some time ago.

By 4 June, Burns was in Dumfries, being made an honorary freeman of the town. Next stop was Dalswinton, to inspect Miller's farm. Finally, on 9 June, he walked unannounced into the family home at Mossgiel. He had been away for more than six months and was received with acclaim, even by the parents of Jean Armour, not that their newly displayed servility pleased Burns. In fact, he was strangely dissatisfied with life at home; too much had happened in his life, in Edinburgh and after, for him to be able to settle back with ease into the old life and into his former occupations.

Soon, Burns' restlessness was finding expression in making plans for going away again. Even the old Jamaica scheme was resurrected, soon to be set aside in favour of a tour, or perhaps several tours, round the Highlands of Scotland.

THE HIGHLAND TOURS

OPPOSITE, TOP
Inveraray Castle, seat of the Duke
of Argyll, Chief of Clan Campbell,
in its fine setting on the edge of
Loch Fyne.

OPPOSITE, BELOW
A closer view of Inveraray Castle.
The building dates from the mid-
18th century and replaced a much
older castle nearby.

Robert Burns made three jour-
neys into the Highlands of
Scotland in the summer and
autumn of 1787. With the Borders tour,
they were to give an unrivalled impetus to
his poet's lyric imagination, offering his
mind and emotions the stimulation of new
scenes, new faces, new music, song and
literature.

His first journey was a short trip into
West Argyll at the end of June. In August
and September came a major expedition: a
600-mile tour of the central Highlands and
north-east Scotland. In early October
there was a shorter trip, taking in Stirling
and Dunfermline, with most of his time
taken up with visits made from
Harvieston House, the home of his friend
Gavin Hamilton's family, which he made
his base.

Robert Burns' first, hastily arranged
Highland tour, to West Argyll, probably
arose out of the frustration of staying at
home on Mossgiel Farm with little to do
and being unable to settle his financial
affairs in Edinburgh. Travelling on horseback (on his hardy little mare, Jenny
Geddes), and not bothering to take his
journal with him, so that we have no
detailed account of this trip, Burns went to
West Argyll by way of Glasgow, where he
may have hoped to increase public aware-
ness of his work, but where he certainly
tried to make his peace with Mary
Campbell's family. Her father, a seaman,
would not meet him, but he did manage to
have an interview with her mother which
may have assuaged his grief and guilt
about the the woman he had promised to
marry after being rejected by Jean

Armour. There is no record at all of
Burns' having visited Mary Campbell's
grave at Greenock, though one or two of
his biographers have suggested that he
would almost certainly have done so.

In Glasgow today there is little trace of
Robert Burns' presence there over two
centuries ago. In the century following his
visit the port changed from a riverside harbour full of sailing ships into one of the
great shipbuilding centres of the world,
with much of the original small town disappearing under the giant shipyards
where most of the world's steel-hulled,
screwdriven ships were being built. It was
this new industry that built the Glasgow
we see today, reclaiming the marshland
which is the centre of the city at George
Square.

Among buildings that remain from an
earlier period is the Cathedral Church of
St Mungo, Glasgow's patron saint. St
Mungo (or Kentigern) is believed to have
built a church here as early as the 6th century. Both the cathedral and the town surrounding it grew in importance after
William the Lion granted a charter in the
12th century. Provand's Lordship, opposite the cathedral, is the oldest house in
Glasgow and dates from about 1471, two
decades or so after Glasgow's university
was founded.

When Burns visited Glasgow in 1787 it
was going through another period of
expansion, boosted by the Industrial
Revolution. George Square, at the heart of
modern Glasgow, had already been laid
out when Burns arrived, with fine
Georgian-style buildings going up round it.
Perhaps it was somewhere round here

that Burns found the silk shop where he bought the elegant fabrics he sent home to his delighted mother and sisters.

Burns left Glasgow for Inveraray via Dumbarton and Loch Lomond, Scotland's largest loch, a route that has become standard for all tourists to this part of Scotland. The road runs along the west side of the lovely, island-strewn loch and there are fine views all the way. After leaving what is today an area of small industries along the River Leven, one comes to the flat meadowlands of the southern edge of Loch Lomond. In Burns' time much of this belonged to the Smollett family, one of whose most famous members was the novelist and travel writer Tobias Smollett, famed for his irascible travel writings on France and Italy.

Today this part of Loch Lomond, with the nearby Trossachs, is a popular sum-

mer holiday area for Glaswegians. The village of Balloch has grown into a resort and offers, among other lake activities, the Balloch Castle Country Park. The original castle here has been reduced to a mound among the trees, the present castle being a 19th-century building housing an information centre.

At this point, Loch Lomond is five miles wide but it narrows towards the north and, as one approaches Tarbet, where Burns made a halt, the peaks of Ben Lomond, at 984 metres (3199 feet) the most southerly of Scotland's Munros, and Ben Vorlich loom close to the loch. From Tarbet there is a road which climbs over a rocky defile to the top of the pass, aptly named in the time of travel on foot or by horse as Rest and be Thankful.

The descent towards Loch Fyne takes the traveller into Campbell country and

Looking up Loch Lomond from Gartocharn, a village at the southern end of the loch. Burns' visit to West Argyll took him up the western shore of Loch Lomond, and back down again. There were several convivial stops on the way, including a 'race' between Burns and his companions and a Highlander on horseback which ended with the riders and their horses all in a heap on the roadway. 'I came off with a few cuts and bruises, and a thorough resolution to be a pattern of sobriety in future,' Burns wrote in a letter to his friend James Smith in Mauchline.

Inveraray, where Burns, after his success in the Borders, expected to be welcomed by the Duke of Argyll, head of Clan Campbell. Unfortunately, the duke was busy entertaining a large party at Inveraray Castle, only recently rebuilt and splendidly redecorated, and hospitality at the local inn, where the innkeeper was kept busy by the duke's guests, was not what Burns had come to expect. Angered by what he took to be an affront, Burns scratched on a window pane

'There's naething here but Highland pride,
And Highland scab and hunger;
If Providence has sent me here,
T'was surely in an anger.'

From Inveraray, Burns went down to Tarbert, at the top of the Kintyre peninsula, then retraced his way via Inveraray and Tarbet to Arrochar, a village at the head of Loch Long which has become a popular touring centre. From here, Burns wrote to his friend Robert Ainslie, describing from a farmer's point of view a very different country from the pleasant land the two had just explored in the Borders. 'I am writing this on my tour through a country where savage streams tumble over savage mountains, thinly overspread with savage flocks, which starvingly support as savage inhabitants,' he wrote. Today, this is still a surprisingly rugged and underpopulated country, considering its relative closeness to Glasgow, but there is nothing savage about its inhabitants, whose welcome to the many tourists who come here from all parts of the world is unfailingly warm and generous.

Burns felt himself to be back in a more civilized world and a politer society at

sures of Dumbarton's Municipal offices.

From Dumbarton, Burns made his way home to Mossgiel Farm at Mauchline, probably by way of Glasgow, Paisley and Kilmarnock.

By early August, Burns was in Edinburgh, where he hoped to settle his financial disagreement with his publisher, William Creech, as well as make the necessary arrangements for his second Highland tour, planned for this month. This time, his companion was to be William Nicol, some 15 years older than Burns and a man of great intellectual ability. He was at this time classics master at Edinburgh High School. This time, the trip was to be in a chaise, not on horseback, and Burns kept up a detailed journal throughout.

The pair set out from Edinburgh on 25 August, making for Falkirk via Linlithgow. The route they followed was almost identical to the one which many travellers to the Highlands still take, except that since there was no Forth bridge on which to cross the river nor a main road to Perth, Burns and Nicol went north via Linlithgow and Falkirk to Stirling, returning via Perth.

On the outskirts of Edinburgh at the Queensferry end of the Forth Bridge a modern traveller with the mobility bestowed by a motorcar can visit two mansions which provide a worthwhile insight into the life of affluent Scots in Burns' day. One of these is Hopetoun House, set in fine parkland on the Firth of Forth. This is one of the finest mansions in Scotland, a splendid example of the work of William Adam and his son John, who expanded and redecorated an older building. The interior decorations with their plaster work and ceilings are fine examples of the style of the period and the collection of paintings by European old masters and the best Scottish painters is noteworthy.

The other house worth a visit is the

Dumbarton, near Glasgow, reached at the end of what was, from Burns's own account of it in a letter to a friend in Mauchline, a lively trip back down Loch Lomondside. This included several hours of singing, dancing and mirth until three in the morning at 'a Highland gentleman's hospitable mansion'. Since the arrival in Dumbarton was followed by another evening of eating and drinking in convivial style, at the end of which 'when we went out to mount our horses, we found ourselves "No verra fou' but gaylie yet"', Burns must have had a fairly heavy head for some time, perhaps even during the ceremony when he was admitted and received as a Burgess and Guild Brother of the burgh of Dumbarton. The Dumbarton Burgess Ticket, presented to Robert Burns on 29 June 1787, and signed by the Town Clerk, is now one of the trea-

This fine bronze statue of Robert Burns stands in Dumbarton Road, in the centre of Stirling. The statue was unveiled in 1914.

House of the Binns, built round a much older house for Thomas Dalyell who made his fortune when he accompanied James VI to London when he succeeded Queen Elizabeth as James I of England in 1603. The house was richly decorated as a result of the owner's new fortune and retains today the fine furniture and plasterwork of the period.

Linlithgow, upriver to the west, possesses the well-preserved ruins of one of Scotland's finest fortified palaces. Linlithgow Palace was visited or lived in by many Scottish monarchs and both James V and his daughter Mary, Queen of Scots were born here. Charles I, who was born in Dunfermline, another very old royal town, thought of making Linlithgow his palace in Scotland. An imposing quadrangle lies at the centre of the palace, surrounded by towers and a wing containing the magnificent Great Hall.

Next to the palace is the Church of St Michael, one of the most interesting parish churches in Scotland. The building is pre-Reformation, having been consecrated in the 13th century and rebuilt after a fire in the 14th century. According to legend, it was here that James IV was warned by an apparition that the coming battle at Flodden would be a disaster.

Linlithgow town has little else of historical interest other than some 17th-century houses; Burns himself, having been shown the room where 'the beautiful injured Mary Queen of Scots was born', commented that, although the royal palace was 'tolerably 'fine', the place itself had 'the appearance of rude, decayed, idle grandeur'.

At Falkirk, too, Burns found little of interest except the tomb of Sir John of Graham but at Bannockburn, two miles south of Stirling, where Robert the Bruce routed the army of Edward II of England in 1314, his imagination took wing. 'Here no Scot can pass uninterested – I fancy to myself that I see my gallant, heroic coun-trymen coming o'er the hill down upon the plunderers of their country, the murderers of their fathers; noble revenge and just hate glowing in every vein...'.

Eventually, Burns' inspiring visit to Bannockburn would find expression in one of his most famous songs, *Scots, Wha Hae*:

> *'Scots, wha hae wi' Wallace bled,*
> *Scots, wham Bruce has aften led,*
> *Welcome to your gory bed*
> *Or to victorie!*

> *'Now's the day, and now's the hour:*
> *See the front o' battle lour,*
> *See approach Proud Edward's power -*
> *Chains and slaverie!...*

> *'Lay the proud usurpers low!*
> *Tyrants fall in every foe!*
> *Liberty's in every blow!*
> *Let us do, or die!'*

Burns was stirred as even the Sassenach visitor is today by the sight of William Wallace's great redoubt at Stirling, which eventually fell to Edward I, to be demolished after the battle of Bannockburn by Robert the Bruce in keeping with his guerrilla war strategy, to use an anachronistic but apt term, against the English. Stirling Castle, towering high above the Forth and the town surrounding it, continued to play a part as a royal residence even when no longer a fortress. James V took refuge here after his father's death at Flodden and Mary, Queen of Scots was crowned Queen of Scotland in the castle at the age of nine months. Her son, James VI, spent his childhood here and in 1745 the castle was unsuccessfully besieged by Bonnie Prince Charlie.

The centre of Stirling is round the Old Burgh Building, with its steeple and a statue of William Wallace. Burns stayed near here, in what was then called James Wingate's Inn and is now the Golden Lion

Hotel, in Quality Street, now King Street.

From here Burns would have had a short walk to the castle, to the north, by way of Spittal Street and St John's Street. At the foot of the castle at this point is the Church of the Holy Rude, in which Mary of Guise was made regent and her grandson crowned James VI. The church is in the Gothic style and the interior has an interesting oak roof and vaulted arches. Above the church is the unfinished palace of the Earl of Mar and beyond it the Esplanade of the castle, today used as a car park, and site of a fine National Trust for Scotland Visitor Centre.

Stirling Castle falls into two sections, the Lower Square and the Upper Square. From the Lower Square one can see the walls of the palace and the Great Hall above and the vaults of the palace kitchens. The Upper Square contains the Palace, Great Hall, Chapel Royal and the King's Old Buildings. Stirling Castle has been much restored and cleaned up, in keeping with its position as a major tourist attraction, but its state of disrepair in 1787 so dismayed Burns that he expressed his disgust with the neglect of this great Scottish monument by scratching this verse on a window pane, using a diamond stylus given him by the Earl of Glencairn:

'Here Stewarts once in triumph reign'd,
And laws for Scotland's weal ordained;
But now unroof'd their Palace stands,
Their sceptre's fall'n to other hands;
Fallen indeed, and to the earth,
Whence grovelling reptiles take their birth.
The injur'd STEWART line are gone,
A race outlandish fills their throne;
An idiot race, to honour lost;
Who knows them best despise them most.'

Two miles from Stirling, on the Forth, was a place that aroused Burns to a more romantic mood. This was Bridge of Allan, a small village which became popular in Victorian times as a spa. Charmed by the

rural atmosphere and the pretty river setting, Burns wrote one of his most famous songs *The Banks of Allan Water,* as a tribute to the place.

From Stirling Burns went along the Ochil hills to Crieff, noting many interesting sights, from the Caldron Linn waterfalls on the River Devon, to the Roman camp called Ardoch in the grounds of Ardoch House, on the way. Until just a few years before his visit, when it was superseded by Stenhousemuir, Crieff had been for centuries one of the chief cattle markets, or 'trysts', of Scotland; today one of its attractive industries is the making of crystal and glass, including paperweights. The town is attractively situated on the River Earn which flows from nearby Loch Earn, whose landscapes are given a

ABOVE
Stirling Castle, one of Scotland's finest examples of military and domestic architecture, combined in one truly royal building, welcomes visitors much more stylishly today than it did in Burns' time.

OPPOSITE
The Wallace Monument rises in the countryside beyond the Old Bridge over the Forth in Stirling. The Old Bridge is a footbridge dating from about 1400 and so is not the bridge, probably a wooden one, which figured in the Battle of Stirling Bridge in 1297, when William Wallace defeated the English army.

special significance by the geological fault which defines the line between Lowland and Highland Scotland. Students of Scottish history will find that the Museum of Tartans in Crieff gives an interesting glimpse of the Scottish clan system.

From Crieff, Burns headed north by way of Kenmore, at the head of Loch Tay, to Aberfeldy. Six miles from Crieff Burns detoured slightly to see Ossian's Stone by the River Almond; the stone is said to mark the grave of the third century Gaelic bard, Ossian. So fine did Burns consider the country round here that he was inspired to pencil a surprisingly lengthy impromptu poem over the chimney-piece of the inn in Kenmore where he stopped:

'... The meeting cliffs each deep-sunk
glen divides,
The woods, wild-scattered, clothe their
ample sides;
Th'outstretching lake, imbosomed 'mong
the hills,
The eye with wonder and amazement fills ...'

Aberfeldy, where the River Tay is joined by Urlar Water, and where it is crossed by one of the finest of the bridges built by General George Wade in his campaigns to pacify the clans after the rebellion of the Old Pretender in 1715, inspired more poetry, this time the fine *The Birks [Birches] of Aberfeldy*:

'Now Simmer blinks on flowery braes,
And o'er the Chrystal streamlets plays;
Come let us spend the lightsome days
In the birks of Aberfeldy.'

Aberfeldy is still a small village of some charm, popular today because it is the key to exploring this part of the Highlands. To the west lies Loch Tay under the lee of Ben Lawers, which separates the loch from the valley of Ben Lyon; to the north lies the glorious valley of Lochs Rannoch and Tummel, linked by rivers whose

waters cascading over boulders in a narrow tree-lined valley provide unforgettable scenery. The waters of the rivers originate on Rannoch Moor to the west and the whole area is wild and beautiful.

From Aberfeldy, Burns and Nicol headed for Dunkeld before turning north for Blair Atholl. The road took them via Grandtully, where the splendid Grandtully Castle was to feature in Walter Scott's *Waverley*, and Logierait, which today is a simple village at the confluence of the Tummel and the Tay but which in Burns' time was known for its prison, from which Rob Roy made a clever escape and which

the Young Pretender later used to keep prisoners taken at Prestonpans.

At Dunkeld, Burns had the great good fortune to meet Neil Gow, the famed Scottish fiddler, spending some time in his house and hearing Gow play. Burns later used many of Gow's Scottish dance tunes for his songs.

While travellers to Blair Atholl today are likely to miss both Grandtully and Logierait, because Blair Atholl is on the A9, the main road through central Scotland, they can follow Burns' route north from Dunkeld. Coming up from Stirling and Perth, the A9 takes in

Pitlochry, a popular resort famed for its drama festivals as well as a salmon ladder which enables the salmon to swim up to their breeding grounds, and the Pass of Killiecrankie, where Graham of Claverhouse, the 'Bonnie Dundee' of the ballads, and his Jacobites (supporters of the recently deposed King James VII and II), defeated the English troops of William III in 1689. The deep, wooded gorge, down which the River Garry tumbles, is a popular beauty spot today in which the ghost of Bonnie Dundee, which so terrifed Hanoverian soldiers during the next generation of Jacobite rebellion, has no place.

Wade's Bridge over the River Tay in Aberfeldy, built between 1733 and 1735. Designed by William Adam, it is one of the finest of the forty bridges built by General George Wade during his great work of putting a proper system of metalled roads and bridges through the Highlands of Scotland in the first half of the 18th century.

North of the Visitor Centre at Killiecrankie, the Claverhouse Stone, marking where Claverhouse fell mortally wounded during the battle, still stands. Burns noted in his journal that he made sure of stopping to see 'the gallant Lord Dundee's stone'.

At Blair Atholl Burns was well received at Blair Castle, supping with the Duchess of Atholl and her family. The Duke had been gradually transforming the old fortress of Blair Castle into an elegant Georgian mansion. The success of the transformation is visible today as one drives up through tall trees to the splendid white buildings whose interior impresses all who visit it. The interior is in 17th- and 18th-century style and there are collections of fine china, tapestries and toys, and portraits of the ancestors of the Murrays of Atholl by such notable painters as Sir Peter Lely, Ramsay, Zoffany and Raeburn.

For Burns, the importance of this visit to Blair Castle lay in his meeting with a Mr Graham of Fintry, who was Commissioner of the Scottish Board of Excise; within a year, Burns would be commissioned into the Excise, providing him with his major source of income for the rest of his life.

From Blair Atholl, Burns and Nicol continued north, making their way towards Fort George and Inverness on the Moray Firth. On 2 September, they were following the Garry river, passing the Falls of Bruar, set in a countryside so treeless that Burns was prompted to write a poem, *The Humble Petition of Bruar Water*, entreating the Duke of Atholl to plant some trees. They dined at Dalwhinnie, where the snow was 17 feet deep on the surrounding hills, crossed the Spey in its spacious valley and so made their way across wild and magnificent country to Aviemore via Ruthven, where the gaunt ruins of the barracks, built to hold Jacobite prisoners, had given shelter to the rem-

Blair Castle, seat of the Duke of Atholl, Chief of the Murray clan, at Blair Atholl. In 1746, before the Battle of Culloden, Blair Castle was beseiged by the advancing Hanoverian troops, thus having the 'honour' of being the last fortress in the British Isles to undergo a seige. Today, the castle still has a ceremonial bodyguard, the Atholl Highlanders, one of whose duties is to provide Guards of Honour for royal visitors to the castle.

Castle Urquhart, whose name translates from Gaelic as 'the fort on the knoll', was once a royal stronghold on the western shore of Loch Ness. It has long been in ruins, which perhaps helps account for the rumour that the Loch Ness Monster's lair is under the castle.

nants of Bonnie Prince Charlie's army after their defeat at Culloden.

The ruins of the barracks are still a landmark for travellers today, and a reminder of the ruthless campaign against the clans. It is a period of Scottish history which seems far removed from the ski resort atmosphere of Aviemore itself with its cluster of fine hotels, shops and leisure amenities. Aviemore began its life as a winter and summer resort in the 1960s and quickly established itself as a place for

winter sports, mountaineering and walking holidays. The main area of activity is to the east in the Cairngorms, reached by the specially built 'ski road' and the Glen More Forest Park, a protected area with forests, small lochs and waymarked paths.

To the east of the Cairngorms lies the lovely valley of the River Dee and the historic village of Braemar with its fine, turreted castle built for a 17th-century Earl of Mar and today owned and lived in by the Farquharsons of Invercauld. Further

avoided by the modern traveller who usually continues on the fast modern road.

Cawdor impressed Burns, who noted without comment in his journal that he was shown the bed in which King Duncan was stabbed. The castle still impresses, for Shakespeare's dramatic account of the murder of Duncan by Macbeth and his wife has created an ineradicable image of the event and the place where, according to Shakespeare, it took place.

About Inverness, which Burns and Nicol reached in the evening of 4 September, Burns had little to say. At this time, the place was a small town with none of the features that interest vistors today. The finest sight in Inverness today, that of the main town over the Ness Bridge on the right bank, with its great castle on a bluff overlooking the river, did not exist in Burns' day for the castle was constructed in the 19th century, as was the Town House, now the town's administrative offices, which dates back only to 1880.

The High Street, which runs from the bridge past the Town House to the east, has some older buildings, including the Steeple of 1791 and the High Church of 1772, which includes the remains of a 14th-century tower. What Inverness lacks in historical interest it makes up for in the liveliness of a market town which is also a touring centre from which visitors can explore the delights of the Great Glen.

Burns' visit to Loch Ness in the Great Glen did not include a search for the Monster which, despite its origins in the time of St Columba, who was said to have saved one of his servants from an attack by some dreadful creature in the loch, did not become a tourist phenomenon until early in this century. Burns did, however, see the ruins of Castle Urquhart which overlooks the loch and is where Nessie has been most often sighted and he enjoyed a supper party at which three young ladies were present, though he does not identify the place where this took

downriver is another famous castle, Balmoral, an estate acquired by Prince Albert and now a favourite home of the Royal Family.

Burns breakfasted at Aviemore, which he thought 'a wild, romantic spot', then, despite the thick snow lying on the surrounding countryside – what today's owners of Aviemore's hotels, guest houses and sports goods shops would give for 18 feet of snow in September! – headed for Inverness via Dulsie and Cawdor, a route

place. Perhaps it was near the Falls of Foyers, which was as far down the eastern shore of Loch Ness that Burns went. The poet found the falls, a splendid cascade of water some 61.5 metres (200 feet) high, impressive enough to write a few *Lines on the Fall of Fyers Near Loch Ness* in pencil on the spot:

'Among the heathy hills and ragged woods
The roaring Fyers pours his mossy floods;
Till full he dashes on the rocky mounds,
Where, thro' a shapeless breach, his stream
resounds...'

The falls are not so impressive in our time because much of the water has been drawn off since late in the 19th century, mainly to power factories and hydro-electric projects.

Burns did not travel any further down the Great Glen, but retraced his steps to Inverness before turning east along the southern coast of the Moray Firth. Burns and Nicol found much to reflect upon as they crossed Culloden Moor, though Burns, who still held unfashionably strong Jacobite sympathies at this time, said little in his journal about the battlefield where the hopes of Bonnie Prince Charlie and the Highlanders who supported him were

finally crushed in April 1746. Though there is little dramatic scenery in this landscape between Nairn and Elgin, the memory of the sad but romantic episode in Scottish history has a strong appeal for visitors, past and present. Today, there is a well-maintained Visitor Centre at Culloden providing plenty of information and souvenirs of Culloden.

From Culloden, Burns went over desolate moors which, his friend Brodie assured him, were still haunted by the witches of Macbeth. Beyond the moors lay Elgin and its impressive ruined cathedral which, for Burns, 'had a grandeur effect at first glance than Melrose, but nothing near so beautiful'.

After crossing the River Spey at Fochabers Burns visited the Duke and Duchess of Gordon at Gordon Castle, on the border of Banff and Moray. Burns was well received by the family, whom he described as 'noble, polite, and generous'. Despite his distrust of the rich and powerful, Burns was always delighted when they treated him, not as a simple ploughman poet of the lower orders, but as an equal.

Burns was now reaching a region of Scotland which had a particularly personal interest for him, for his father had come from here. Taking the road to Banff, where he noted the improvements in agriculture, he went for a ride along the shore and visited Duff House, designed by William Adam, and also passed Boyne Castle at Portsoy Bay. From Banff, Burns and Nicol went across the moorland south of the River Newby by way of Deer, where Burns noted that both land and crops were rich, to Peterhead, then south via Slains Castle and Ellon to Aberdeen, where Burns was looking forward to meeting aunts, uncles and cousins and to seeing for himself the land from which his father had sprung.

Writing to his brother Gilbert, Burns said, 'I spent two days among our rela-

The ruins of Arbroath Abbey in Arbroath, on the North Sea coast of Angus. Robert Burns came into Arbroath by sailing ship near the end of his great Highlands tour. The short sea trip from Auchmithie, three miles up the coast, did not upset him, for he noted that, once ashore, he dined and then visited the 'stately ruins' of the Abbey.

now incorporated into the splendid Victorian Town House. Aberdeen chose not to feel slighted by Burns, putting up a statue of him in 1892.

Today, while Aberdeen takes pride in being the anything-but-lazy 'Oil Capital of Europe', it is also quick to emphasize its other attractions, from the ancient buildings at the centre of the 'granite city', to the fine salmon rivers and golf courses which abound in the Grampian region, along with a fine concentration of whisky distilleries and fifty per cent of all the prehistoric standing stones in Scotland.

The east coast south of Aberdeen is rich in castles, among them Dunnottar, near Stonehaven, where Burns thought the coast 'a good deal romantic'. The extensive ruins of Dunnottar Castle, built on the site of a Pictish fort, are spread across a dramatic promontory around which the restless sea breaks in a white tracery of spray.

From Stonehaven, Burns and Nicol turned inland, making an overnight stop at Laurencekirk, a market town at the centre of an area of Kincardineshire fertile farming land known as the Howe of Mearns. They then turned towards the coast again, which they reached at Montrose, a quiet town by the tidal basin of the Montrose lagoon which was fought over many times and in 1716 saw the secret departure of the Old Pretender for exile in France. From here, they chose to sail down the wild rocky coast, looking out for the several famous caverns in the cliffs, before landing at the historic royal burgh of Arbroath, whose finest hour had come in 1320 when the Estates of Scotland came here to declare their independence of the English crown and acknowledge Robert Bruce as king of Scotland.

Today a holiday resort and famous for its kippers, Arbroath was noted in Burns' time more for the ruins of its fine sandstone abbey, built by William the Lion and dedicated to the murdered Thomas à

tives, and found our aunts, Jean and Isbal, still alive and hale old women, John Caird, though born the same year as our father, walks as vigorously as I can; they have had several letters from his son in New York, – William Brand is likewise a stout old fellow.'

From now on, Burns' journey was more hurried than he would have liked for William Nicol was impatient to complete the tour and return to Edinburgh. The modern traveller may prefer to explore more slowly along Scotland's east coast, which is full of beauty and history.

Aberdeen itself, set between two fine rivers, the Dee and the Don, is worth much more than the glance Burns gave it as he hurried through to meet his relations: 'a lazy town', he remarked in his journal, having spent one night there, at the New Inn in Castle Street right in the centre of town near the notable Mercat Cross and the old tolbooth, once a prison,

Becket. The abbey has connections with the Incheape Rock which lies offshore, for one of its abbots placed the warning bell to shipping on it which gave the rock its alternative name, Bell Rock.

In Dundee, 'a lowlying and pleasant town', Burns spent much of his time visiting friends and admirers, one of the main purposes of his tours. He then went on, 'thro the rich harvests and fine hedge rows of the carse of Gowrie' to Perth, once the capital of Scotland and today a city of many attractions stretching along the banks of the River Tay.

Scene of many a fight between Scots and English, Perth was also an important centre of religious life; the White, Black and Grey friars had monasteries here and John Knox preached in Perth's St John Church his famous Reformation sermon.

The city has two fine riverside parks, the North Inch and South Inch, the latter a fine green space whose open air entertainments today are a far cry from the witch burnings which once took place here. The North Inch is surrounded by fine houses, including Balhousie Castle, originally built in 1422 and now housing the Black Watch Museum, and the Fair Maid of Perth's House, named after Walter Scott's romantic tale.

While in Perth, Burns took time to visit Scone Palace, built on the site of an ancient abbey and palace destroyed in 1559 by a mob inflamed by John Knox's Reformation sermon. Burns noted particularly a picture of the Chevalier (Bonnie Prince Charlie) and his sister and Queen Mary's bed, which impressed him because the hangings were 'made by her own hands'. The Scone Palace which today's visitor sees is not the same as the building of Burns' day, for it was rebuilt in a castellated style early in the 19th century. Scone is today the seat of the earls of Mansfield.

From Perth, Burns and Nicol headed south, coming, Burns' journal ends, 'through a cold barren Country to Queensferry – dine – cross the ferry and come to Edinburgh'. It was 16 September. In a letter written a day later to his brother Gilbert, Burns noted that their tour had taken 22 days and that they had travelled 600 miles, 'windings included'. He outlined the places he had visited, but ended by saying 'The rest of my stages are not worth rehearsing – warm as I was from Ossian's country where I had seen his very grave, what car'd I for fisher-towns and fertile Carses?'.

Burns was to make one more trip back to the central Highlands before he gave up his 'touring', spending rather more than two weeks in Stirlingshire during October 1787. As with his first Highlands tour, Burns did not keep a journal, and much of our knowledge of the trip comes from the account written by Burns' travelling companion, Dr James Adair, a friend from Ayr. Several days were spent at the Hamilton family home, Harvieston, where Dr Adair met Mrs Hamilton's eldest daughter, whom he later married. There were visits to Stirling and Dunfermline, where Burns and Adair visited the abbey and Burns knelt at the flagstone supposed to mark the grave of Robert the Bruce, kissing it fervently.

Montrose, built on a tongue of land between the North Sea and a tidal lagoon called the Montrose Basin. The town, which Burns thought a 'finely situated handsome town', saw the departure of Sir James Douglas for the Holy Land, carrying with him the heart of Robert the Bruce, and, in much gloomier circumstances in 1716, the departure of the Old Pretender after the failed Jacobite Rising of 1715.

EXCISEMAN IN DUMFRIES AND GALLOWAY

In 1788 came a watershed year for Robert Burns. In February, after a second winter in Edinburgh during which his passionate but platonic relationship with Mrs Agnes MacLehose, the 'Clarinda' of some of his finest poetry, had waxed and waned, Burns returned to Mauchline. Within a week he and Jean Armour were living together, thus publicly testifying that they were indeed man and wife. The following month, Jean gave birth to twin daughters, both of whom died within weeks.

Not long after this, Burns signed a lease on the farm at Ellisland near Dumfries which his friend Patrick Miller had offered him. In April, Burns began receiving instruction in the duties of an Excise officer at Mauchline, in the hope of being appointed to this occupation as a result of his meeting with Mr Graham of Fintry at Blair Atholl. By June, he was settled in Ellisland, though Jean did not join him until the end of the year, and in July his Excise commission was issued. Burns was to continue struggling to farm the unyielding land at Ellisland until the end of 1791, mainly because his duties as an Excise officer, which he took up in 1789, did not of themselves provide enough for the Burns family to live on.

The Edinburgh publication of his poems and of the *Scots Musical Museum* had brought him literary acclaim but no financial stability, while his tours of Scotland had not brought him the financial success for which he had hoped. Burns had had to accept early on that he would have to make his living by other means than his poetry. Although he would return to Edinburgh on several occasions, his departure from the capital in 1788 was tinged with regret but also accompanied by some relief. He had realized that to many of his noble and influential friends he had remained a curiosity, a peasant ploughman with a gift for verse and that he would never be accepted on their social level. His natural pride and his passionate belief in the equality of men made him rebel against this circumstance as much as his hatred of hypocrisy and cant. He was sorry, of course, to part from his true friends, among them Agnes MacLehose and Mrs Dunlop. Mrs MacLehose, whom he had addressed in his many letters to her as Clarinda while signing himself Sylvander, was in any case leaving for America to join her husband. The idyll was over and Burns was left to record his feelings in poetry:

'Had we ne'er loved so kindly,
Had we ne'er loved so blindly
Never met or never parted
We had ne'er been broken hearted.'

At Dumfries, Burns decided to turn over a new leaf. His home there with Jean was a permanent thing, with Jean, a remarkably forgiving woman, undertaking the care of at least one of Robert's illegitimate children as well as her own. As always, Burns expressed his resolution in poetry:

'I hae a wife o'my ain,
I'll partake wi' naebody;
I'll tak cuckold frae nane.
I'll gie cuckold to naebody.'

But, to quote Burns himself (in *To A Mouse*), 'The best laid schemes o' mice and men Gang aft agley'. On a visit to Edinburgh early in 1789, Burns was settling two matters of business, his accounts with William Creech and a suit by a girl called Jenny Clows, who had given birth to Burns' son three months earlier. Then, in March 1791, an affair between Burns and a girl called Anna Park resulted in the birth of their daughter Elizabeth, less than two weeks before Jean gave birth to their son, William Nicol Burns.

The 170-acre farm at Ellisland, in the valley of the River Nith six and a half miles north of Dumfries on the A76, is still a working farm today. The farmhouse in which Burns lived for three years and where he wrote many popular works, including *Auld Lang Syne* and *Tam O' Shanter*, is open to the public and has exhibitions of Burnsiana and agricultural life.

Robert Burns' career in the Excise paid him £50 a year, with a similar bonus paid on the apprehension of smugglers and other Excise breakers. In the pursuit of his duties he rode some 200 miles a year through Dumfries and Galloway, check-ing on tradesmen and shopkeepers to ensure that the multitudinous and complex duties were being paid. In 1793 and 1794 he also made short tours of the region similar to his Borders and Highlands tours of 1787. There are guides available to the Dumfries and Galloway tours, allowing Burns' admirers to stay in the inns he stayed in and to read for themselves the many poems and songs he wrote while there. At the Selkirk Arms Hotel in Kirkcudbright, for instance, he wrote the *Selkirk Grace*, and a stay in the Murray Arms Hotel at Gatehouse of Fleet resulted in the rousing *Scots, Wha Hae*.

Burns gave up the struggle with the Ellisland farm in the late summer of 1791, auctioning off his crops and making a formal renunciation of the lease. He moved his family into Dumfries to a house at 11 Bank Street, then known as the Wee Vennel, where Robert, Jean and their three sons had three small rooms on the second floor. Later, they moved into a larger residence at 24 Burns Street, then called Millbrae Vennel, where in addition to his own children by Jean Armour Burns took in his illegitimate daughter by

is a bas relief showing Dumfries as it was in Burns' day. Just off the High Street is the Globe Inn, dating from 1610, whose snuggery was Burns' howff (meeting place). Here is kept the chair that Burns occupied during the many convivial evenings he spent in the tavern. The Hole in the Wa', another of Burns' haunts in Dumfries, also has some Burns memorabilia. Around a corner to the south-west is Burns Street. Number 24, where the poet and his family lived from 1792 and where Burns died in 1796, is now a museum carefully restored to its late 18th-century condition and with a good collection of Burns' manuscripts and memorabilia.

The southern end of Burns Street joins St Michael's Street where St Michael's Church is situated. In its graveyard stands the Greek-style mausoleum where Burns, his wife and some of their children are buried. A stone pedestal has been put up in the churchyard indicating the locations of the graves of other people associated with Burns in Dumfries, including his good friend James McLure.

From St Michael's Church it is a short walk to the river, a part of Dumfries where the poet was perhaps reminded of his childhood in Ayrshire, for the Nith has a six-arched old footbridge and a weir and the sort of quiet seclusion he liked to get away to to let poetical ideas rise to the surface of his mind. A fine Robert Burns Centre, complete with an audio-visual theatre illustrating Robert Burns' life in Dumfries, was opened in the old Town

ABOVE AND ABOVE RIGHT No. 24 Burns Street, the house in Dumfries which was Burns' last home, and a corner of a room inside the house. Burns and his family lived here from 1792 until his death in 1796, Jean Armour remaining in the house until her own death in 1834. Today, the house has been carefully restored and is a fine museum devoted to Robert Burns' life and work.

Anna Park. Jean Armour was to live in this house until her death in 1834.

Dumfries was a sizeable town on the Nith even in Burns' day, with the usual war-torn history of most towns near the Border. A royal burgh since the time of William the Lion, Dumfries had been attacked by Edward I and several times burned and sacked by the forces of other English kings and army commanders. It was even damaged by the forces of Bonnie Prince Charlie retreating from Derby.

For the modern visitor tracing Burns' life in Dumfries, a walk in the town has plenty to offer. Starting at Castle Street and passing Burns' statue outside the Greyfriars Church, which was built on the site of the old castle, one comes to Midsteeple, the town centre where Castle Street joins the High Street. In Midsteeple

Mill on the riverside in 1986.

The visitor exploring Burns territory in Nithsdale will find a quiet road from Dumfries up to Thornhill, where Burns used to have his footwear repaired. The cobbler's shop has now been replaced by a hotel but the village is still as tranquil a place as when Burns strolled there or later when Kirkpatrick Macmillan rode through it on his newly invented chain-driven bicycle. For Burns, the avid collector of Scottish verse and songs, the area round Thornhill had another interest for it was near here, at Maxwelton House near Moniaive, that the original Annie Laurie, of the ballad written by William Douglas, lived.

North of Thornhill is one of Scotland's great castles, Drumlanrig, near the village of Carronbridge. The site has been occupied since Roman times but what the visitor sees today is a 17th-century mansion built in the local pink sandstone with corner towers for the 1st Duke of Queensberry. The interior is as impressive as the outside and contains a gallery of paintings by old masters including Rembrandt, Holbein, Murillo and Ruysdael. Among the fine furniture is a piece presented by Charles II to his illegitimate son, the Duke of Monmouth, who was married to the daughter of the Duke of Buccleuch. Beyond Carronbridge the A76 goes on into Ayrshire and the countryside of Burns' childhood.

During his Border tour of 1787, Burns had glimpsed something of the Dumfries and Galloway countryside, but his work as an Excise collector enabled him to get to know it much better, from Gretna on the Border to Sanquhar and Moffat in the north and to Newton Stewart, Gatehouse of Fleet and Kirkcudbright in the south and west.

Memories of his Borders tour must have made him smile at Gretna Green, for instance, where he must surely have remembered the girl who had tried to per-

suade him to take her to the marriage smithy, where a lifelong commitment could be arranged in minutes. Until 1940, marriage by declaration such as Burns had committed himself to with Jean Armour and Mary Campbell was still valid in Scotland and attracted thousands of young men and women from all over Britain to Gretna Green. Today, this is

Summer in Nithsdale, Dumfrieshire, and the hay has been harvested and baled. Although farming is now a machine-oriented business, the countryside remains inextricably imprinted with images of Burns's poetry, of his struggles with the unyielding earth, of his love affairs and of his silent and private meditations on life which found expression in his poetry.

just a memory but still a potent one for tourists who visit the Old Smithy and its museum.

There are other attractions for visitors in the area too, one being the cave at Kirkpatrick which, with caves in other places, claims to be the one where Robert the Bruce had his fighting spirit restored by watching a spider repeatedly rebuild its shattered web. The cave, once only accessible by climbing down a rope, can now be reached by a path.

For vistors with literary interests Ecclefechan, inland from the coastal town of Annan, is worth visiting for this was the birthplace of Thomas Carlyle whose home, Arched House, is now a museum. Burns knew both Annan and Ecclefechan well, for his Excise duties took him there often. At Annan he lodged at a house in the High Street which is now the Café Royal, dashing off *The Deil's awa wi th' Exciseman* on one visit. At Ecclefechan

Burns was caught in the great snow-storm of 6-8 February 1795. It may have been during this enforced stay that he made the fine sketch of a church plus a few lines of verse, signed R. Burns, which were uncovered during a recent refurbishment of the Selkirk Arms hotel, called the Heid Inn in Burns' day.

North-west of Ecclefechan is Lochmaben, which Burns visited regularly and where a close friend was the town provost, Robert Maxwell. Burns often stayed with the town's minister, the Rev. Andrew Jaffray, whose 15-year-old daughter was the original 'Blue-eyed Lassie'.

Robert Maxwell may well have been a member of the great Border family, the Maxwells, whose domain was in this part of Dumfries and Galloway, with their greatest stronghold being Caerlaverock Castle on the coast west of Annan. The Maxwells' greatest rivals were the Johnsons of nearby Lockerbie, notorious for slashing the faces of their enemies leaving scars which came to be known as the 'Lockerbie lick'.

The land across the Nith estuary south of Dumfries was a stewartry land, so-called because the historic overlords, the Balliols and the Douglases, had their over-lordships annulled in the 15th century, a royal steward being appointed instead. To the south of Dumfries along the A710 is Sweetheart Abbey, also known as New Abbey. The ruined abbey was originally built on the orders of Devorguilla Balliol, wife of the John Balliol who was Regent of Scotland while Alexander III was a boy. After her husband's death Devorguilla took his heart, keeping it with her until her own death when she was buried with it before the high altar in the Abbey.

The region in the west of Galloway was one which Burns only came to know well in 1793 and 1794, when he undertook his two tours in the area, in the company of his closest friend in Dumfries, John Syme, who also worked for the Excise. Among the places they are known to have visited were Kirkcudbright, Gatehouse of Fleet and Newton Stewart, all of them linked today by the main road in the south, the A75.

Kirkcudbright, named after St Cuthbert, lies where the River Dee flows into Kirkcudbright Bay on the Solway Firth. Once a royal burgh and stewartry capital, Kircudbright is today an attractive town and a place long favoured by artists. There are few old buildings of tourist interest other than the Mercat Cross and the Tolbooth, but there is a Museum of Stewartry and Broughton House has displays of Burnsiana. Less than six miles from Kirkcudbright is Dundrennan Abbey, now a ruin, where Mary, Queen of Scots spent her last hours in Scotland, incognito and with her red hair shorn to escape detection, while she awaited word that her cousin Queen Elizabeth would give her sanctuary in England. The word

never came and eventually the desperate Scottish queen set out impetuously across the Solway Firth to Cumberland where all that awaited her was twenty years of imprisonment in England, ended by her execution in 1587.

For the holiday visitor the south-west corner of Scotland has attractions of a fine sea coast and beautiful inland landscapes. To the north of the region is the Galloway Forest Park, a hilly, wooded region with abundant wildlife where several of the region's rivers have their sources. Newton Stewart, where Burns is known to have visited Kirroughtree House (now a hotel), makes a good base from which to explore Galloway Forest Park. At the extreme south-western point is the hammerhead peninsula known as the Rhinns of Galloway, where there is fine coastal scenery; at the northern head of the hammer is Loch Ryan, with the ferry port for Ireland at Stranraer and at the southern head is the Mull of Galloway with dramatic cliffs and seabird life. Portpatrick, about halfway down the western coast of the

Sweetheart Abbey, among the most romantic of the ruined castles and abbeys which remain as evocative reminders of past history in Dumfries and Galloway. The abbey, whose ruins lie south of Dumfries on the A710, was founded in 1273 by John Balliol's wife, Dervorguilla, after he was killed by Robert the Bruce. When she died, aged 90, her body and her husband's heart were interred together in the abbey's church.

79

Rhinns of Galloway, was the home of Burns' friend, John Gillespie; the statue of Burns near the village bowling green was erected in 1929.

After his return from his second tour of Galloway, Burns' health and fortunes took a turn for the worse. His illness, which may have been rheumatic fever, made him too weak to write and he was anxious about his loss of income from the Excise as well as sundry debts. The debts, including one to his tailor, were small, but preyed on his mind and he feared persecution and the debtors' prison. Jean was pregnant again and the thought of the future of his family tormented him. Moreover, he was no longer the hero of rich Edinburgh admirers, partly because of his bawdy poems and tavern company and partly because he had been under suspicion for sedition after the French Revolution, because of what would be called today his left-wing sympathies. In 1792, although he had been made an honorary member of the Royal Company of Archers in Edinburgh, he also had to undergo an Excise inquiry into his loyalty at the end of the year. The next year, however, France declared war on Britain, and Burns made it clear that he was no traitor; by 1795 he was even helping organize the Dumfries Volunteers.

At the end of this year, he was ill again, however, and would never be well again. He put himself in the hands of Dr Maxwell, regarded as a desperate measure at a time when doctors knew little and were distrusted by everybody. Dr Maxwell recommended immersion in the waters of the Solway Firth — this for a man suffering from rheumatic fever and possibly angina. Burns also several times visited the Brow Well, an ancient mineral well at the village of Ruthwell, south of Dumfries, to take the waters there.

Burns died in Dumfries on 21 July 1796. His funeral, arranged by John Syme, was a grand military affair. Because he had joined the Dumfries Volunteers, he was given a guard of honour and the procession was also accompanied by two regiments that were temporarily stationed at Dumfries. On the day of the funeral, Jean Armour gave birth to her ninth child, a boy who was called Maxwell.

For the casual visitor to Scotland today, Robert Burns may seem just another romantic figure in a holiday landscape, set up beside Mary, Queen of Scots, John Knox and Bonnie Prince Charlie as protagonists in a tourist attraction, wrapped in tartan and their faces printed on tins of shortbread biscuits. Few non-Scots who visit the guide book places will have read much of his poetry and to many, as in his own time, his character will be that of a wild, undisciplined peasant ploughman with a gift for light poetry.

Read a little deeper, however, and Robert Burns becomes one of those rare creatures, a natural genius with an extraordinary passion for life. In this sense he can be compared with Vincent van Gogh. Neither man had a disciplined education, but both sought out the information they needed to further their creative aims. Both of them had a powerful earthy emotional drive which was the engine of their creativity and both of them remained free and uncompromising in the face of the stereotyping which the pressures of society impose on most of us.

Burns also had an intense patriotism, a real passion for the land and people to which he belonged. Almost singlehanded he kept alive the songs and verse and speech that were disappearing under the influence of a more standard English. He was the embodiment of his people and his recognition world-wide suggests that he was also the soul of the individuality that lies at the centre of all human beings.